A LIFE

Morris Clegg, 1998.

A LIFE

Morris Clegg

iUniverse, Inc.

New York Lincoln Shanghai

A LIFE

Copyright © 2005 by Morris Clegg

iUniverse books may be ordered through booksellers or by contacting:

iUniverse
2021 Pine Lake Road, Suite 100
Lincoln, NE 68512
www.iuniverse.com
1-800-Authors (1-800-288-4677)

ISBN: 0-595-34300-7 (pbk)
ISBN: 0-595-67099-7 (cloth)

Printed in the United States of America

To Judy.

Whose love and support has sustained me for almost half a century.

Morris

Contents

Foreword

It must be supposed that when someone sets out to write anything at all, the author has in mind a target readership. In my case that is easily resolved—it is my children and grandchildren. Parents generally know quite a lot about their children, although possibly not as much as they would like! Children however know much less about their parents. These pages may, in some measure, help to level the playing field.

Children begin by seeing the parent as an all wise, all knowing, all protective figure, the one who has an answer to every problem, able to heal every hurt. Only gradually are these comfortable illusions dispelled, like the removing of the seven veils. Finally they see parents for what they really are, every bit as fallible as are the children themselves! Though by the time they have fully discovered this, they won't be children any longer.

Unlike many activities, and ones of immeasurably less importance, there are no degree courses in parenting. Each comes to it with a total lack of experience, save that girls sometimes may have helped mother with her younger siblings. Boys on the other hand routinely want any and all pertinent knowledge. In these circumstances parents have no option but to learn on their feet. They must hope that by the time their offspring are beginning to question, they will have learnt sufficient to be able to stand up to an increasingly challenging scrutiny. Children for their part have no alternative but to be the raw material for their parents' practice! In recompense for being required to adopt this uncertain role, they need to know that they have every opportunity to note where and how their parents are getting it wrong. This will ensure that in their own turn they won't make the same mistakes with their children.

They will he wise not to assume that this will result in a trouble free upbringing of their own offspring, for nothing is more certain than that their children will find a whole new set of faults to lay to the charge of their parents. And so on down the generations. It will be apparent from this that perhaps the most important decision any child will ever make is the choosing of its parents!

Such a memoir as this must be an intensely personal matter in which the pronoun 'I' is disproportionately present. It isn't a complete story of my life, but is, I believe, an essentially accurate one within its compass. Nor do I deceive myself that it might have an appeal beyond the most limited circle. But it was fun doing it.

Morris Clegg

EARLIEST DAYS

My life began in 1930, May 6th, to be precise. It was not a particularly auspicious time to arrive. The Western world was struggling with a very deep slump that wrecked the German currency, caused havoc in her economy and produced millions of unemployed, and called into question the future of capitalism. All of which was the harbinger for one Adolf Hitler. It was ominous that in that year, Hitler's party, the National Socialists (Nazis), made large electoral gains, returning 107 members to the Reichstag. Here in Great Britain too—the U.K. hadn't been invented—unemployment soared, and for most, money was hard to come by. The United States was sunk in the deepest depression she had ever known. The R101 airship crashed on its maiden flight killing most on board, and effectively put paid to British pursuit of lighter than air travel. The Germans were to plod on with their Zeppelins until the Hindenburg was destroyed by fire at Lakehurst in America.

Noel Coward put his play *Private Lives* on the London stage with great success. Sigmund Freud wrote *Civilisation and its Discontents* and was gaining world recognition for his rather singular, and usually mistaken, interpretation of human behaviour. The film *All Quiet on the Western Front* won an Academy Award. The BBC Symphony Orchestra was formed, whilst Pluto (not Disney!) was discovered, and added to the other eight planets of the solar system. Australia had a good year in cricket—some things just don't change!—with Donald Bradman scoring 334 runs in the Leeds Test Match. That's more than England usually manages to clock up in a whole innings! And France began to build her Maginot Line, reflecting her sense of insecurity. In the event it wasn't going to do her much good.

We still had the empire about which hardly anybody had begun to feel uncomfortable, rather a sense of pride that we were taking civilisation to "lesser breeds without the law". As schoolchildren we looked at the globe, having been taught that everything in red was ours—and there was a lot of red! Ruling over such a large slice of the world from so small a base—Great Britain didn't look very great on the map—surely had to mean we were a very special nation. It was something to be proud of, and it seemed reasonable to suppose it would continue forever. As King George V lay dying in January 1936, one of the last things he said to Lord Wigram, his Principal Private Secretary, was, "How is the Empire?'—to which Wigram responded, "All is well, Sir, with the Empire."

But was it? Beneath the surface was a seething mass of discontents. The subject peoples of the empire were not, despite what we were taught, grateful for our governance of them—they just wanted us out. Though once having succeeded in just that, whether what followed was an improvement must be thought very questionable. With almost the whole of Africa now a basket case, having suffered uniformly dreadful leaders in the mould of Idi Amin, Mobuto, Mugabe *et al*, sovereignty has done less than nothing for the vast majority of the peoples of that hapless continent. Uncounted millions have died in the unending wars, millions more from famine, and yet more millions from unchecked disease, led by AIDS.

Germany was beginning to flex her muscles and loathed the Versailles Treaty imposed on her eleven years previously. She too had known hunger, following the humiliating defeat of 1918 and the misery that followed the total collapse of her currency. Massive unemployment throughout the West made millions lose confidence in capitalism and look for alternatives. Many believed Communism was the only way forward, and sought to promote it in their own countries, but did so because the famine in Russia, deliberately engineered by Stalin to break the resistance of the peasantry to collectivisation, and the terror that was raging wherever his writ ran, had not become common knowledge.

None of this in 1930 gave me the slightest pause for thought, nor made me wonder whether it had been wise to make an appearance at that exact moment! All seemed reasonably well in my small world in those early years. My older sister and I had enough to eat; we even had ice cream once or twice a year—a substantial treat. We felt secure in the care of our parents, and quarrelled as frequently as any other siblings. There were periods of non-belligerency, usually of short duration, for points of difference were not hard to find! It was demonstrated by us, and further down the line by our own children, and more recently still by our grandchildren, that there is only one toy in this world that any child wants to play with, and that is the toy the other child has.

School days didn't begin until the age of five, though some of my peers went to local pre-school gatherings, organised by enterprising individuals. My first school was the kindergarten section of the same Cowley School that my sister attended, and involved about a four mile journey on a tram that clanged its way along rails, rails which were a potential hazard to cyclists with the possibility of their wheels getting stuck in the grooves. Some of the older trams were open to the weather on top, so on fine days it was more fun to be upstairs. It was quite a grown up feeling to be fitted out with a school uniform, complete with cap and satchel for books, and in which lunch was carried. Though often accompanied by my sister, there were many times when I travelled solo. The idea that one should be accompanied by an adult would have been considered totally unnecessary. Statistically, the chances of a child being abducted or interfered with now are almost identical with the position seventy years ago. The perception however is very different today. My recollection of lessons is, on the whole, positive. There was a firm emphasis on the three 'R's', but academics were not all we learnt. Pinned to the mantelpiece in the classroom were five brightly coloured squares, each a different shade. Every day, at the beginning of the first lesson, we all had to show our handkerchiefs. If just one pupil failed to produce one, down came the square for that day in a solemn little ritual, to be interred in the teacher's desk. It wasn't long before every child had a handkerchief without fail! To this day I would never go anywhere without a clean one!

Not very popular with the boys was the practice of a short period of rest after lunch. Folding canvas beds were brought out, and we were required to lie down on these for perhaps twenty minutes. No one went to sleep, and it didn't really fit the macho male image. My first schoolmistress was a very imaginative teacher. She was always devising ways to capture our attention. Our early introduction to adding and subtracting would involve strategies such as chairs formed into lines, with one child acting the part of bus conductor, complete with tickets, money bag, and the punch machine in use in those days. The rest would be passengers tendering their fare using cardboard, but quite realistic looking money. If the conductor didn't give the right change he lost his job! The passenger who recognised his change was wrong became the conductor. We all hoped desperately to be given the wrong change!

After three years of kindergarten, we graduated to the boys' junior school, involving a longer bus ride and walk. Housed in a Victorian mansion, there were just three forms to serve the three-year period before moving on to the senior school. The school part was on the ground floor. The first floor was the home of the headmaster of the senior school. Tall, lean and angular, immaculately dressed in a sober business suit, Gerry Dowse was the quintessential picture of a school head, even down to the *pince nez* through which he would look piercingly at any who crossed his path.

The first year was only for eight-year-old boys. The girls by this time had disappeared. We were taught by a lady of ample girth, a Miss Moore. Much given to makeup, she was very much in charge—not a lady to he treated lightly. One much favoured method of sharing her knowledge with any who appeared to be slow on the uptake, was to take an exercise book and steadily strike the recalcitrant on the head in time to the driving home of the point at issue. This was not thought to be too severe—it produced more sound than pain. The real penalty was to be sent to the headmaster. This invariably meant a caning, and *that* hurt. It was important however not to cry, or else face would be lost with one's peers.

Second year students moved up to Billy Hayes, a significant development, for it was the first time we were taught by a man. Had it not been for the war, all our teachers from here on would have been male. He was an easy-going chap who has left but little impression, though no doubt he was a competent teacher.

Final year, ten year olds, were under the eagle eye of the head, 'Daddy' Kermode. Always smartly turned out, and wearing a gown at all times, he was not to be trifled with. This was the man who wielded the cane, which hung behind the blackboard. He was never unwilling to use it if needs be, a fact of which we were fully aware. No doubt today he and his staff would he hung, drawn and quartered. That today's approach is all gain, however, must be much in doubt. The teacher then was in control. His or her time was therefore spent exclusively on teaching, not on trying to maintain order. The child paid attention. Failure to do so incurred severe disincentives. The benign result was that effective learning was the norm, and exam standards didn't have to be manipulated down to ensure an adequate level of 'success'.

The Western world generally is passing through a quite extraordinary phase, loosely understood as 'political correctness'. This intrudes into school life as well as a host of other areas. In the event of a schoolchild being saddened perhaps by the loss of someone he or she loves, the teacher, willing to share the pain, might very properly put an arm round the child and give it a hug and offer some kindly words of understanding. But 'no, no!' cry the witch finders—this constitutes an 'assault' or 'abuse' of the child, an invasion of its space! What nonsense! The only thing being abused in such a situation is the English language. In due time the innate common sense of the British people will surely re-assert itself, and these bizarre responses relegated to a scornful footnote in history. In the meantime children, and many others, are the losers.

SCHOOL IN WARTIME

Having passed through the two preliminary stages of a Cowley School education, it was time to move on to the senior school. By now war had broken out, and we carried our gas masks everywhere we went. Masters began to disappear into the services and women took their place. This produced an animated discussion as to the proper mode of address; for such, 'Miss' was ruled out, if only because hardly any of them were. 'Ms' hadn't been invented. 'Ma'am' was thought to be trespassing on royal territory, if not prerogatives. 'My lady' wasn't even considered! And so 'Madam' was the final choice.

A first impression of the senior school was size. Previously we had known nothing beyond about a hundred pupils. Here there were six times that number and with buildings to match, all complete with purpose built art rooms, woodworking shops and laboratories—initially a bit intimidating, the more so as all the boys, our own year excepted, were bigger and stronger. Whilst we had from the outset been subject to a moderately firm level of discipline, under Mr Dowse this was significantly enhanced. It extended beyond the school confines. Any boy in school uniform and not wearing his cap was committing a grievous offence, as was eating in the street. Within the school exacting standards were set and upheld; any threat to them was dealt with firmly.

Truancy, now so large a problem with literally thousands of our children roaming the streets every single school day despite patrols to redirect them back to school, just didn't exist at Cowley. I have no recollection of a single boy even considering or attempting it. Certainly the Head would have made an example of any such offender!

There was one female teacher, young and inexperienced, who took us for history. We sensed an opportunity to take advantage. Boys given an inch will unhesitatingly take a foot! Word reached Mr Dowse. The classroom layout was round a quadrangle, with a cloister giving access, and each classroom had windows along its length on the cloister side. The head approached our classroom from behind, so we didn't see him. He waited out of our sight, just long enough to satisfy himself that what he had heard was true. He came into the room and caned every boy on the spot. My recollection is that we got four each. With over thirty of us, that must have been quite an exercise! When not in use his cane slipped neatly into a bespoke pocket of his immaculate gown. The teacher in question—her name escapes me—left shortly after that. Mr Dowse brooked no breach of his standards.

When there was a particularly serious setback in the progress of the war, the headmaster would call the whole school to assemble in the hall and spell out the detail of the disaster and the implications of it. One occasion registered very firmly in my mind. This was the fall of Singapore and the sinking of two of our best battleships, one of which was the *Prince of Wales*, a brand new and very powerful ship. Singapore had been believed to be impregnable and was held to be the key to our power and empire in the Far East. The Japanese took it with surprising ease, and sank our ships with their aircraft. It was attacked from the land, thought by the British to be impossible. So much so, that all the defensive guns pointed only to the sea and couldn't be trained on the land to their rear. It was to prove to be the beginning of the end of our Far Eastern possessions, for even though in the end we won the war, we never recovered our earlier influence there. It also heralded the demise of the battleship as a weapon of war. They were too costly to build and maintain, and too exposed to aerial warfare. Their strength and days of glory lay in sea battles before the advent of airpower.

On another occasion we were solemnly gathered together to be told of the loss of the battlecruiser *H.M.S. Hood*. This was not just another capital ship—it was the pride and supreme symbol of British sea power. Her building was ordered in 1916 after the Battle of Jutland, and at 45,000 tons was the largest and most powerful ship in the navy. Between the wars she sailed to all parts of the empire, showing the flag and visibly demonstrating the power of Great Britain. Her loss was an equally visible proof of just how uncertain that power was. The damage to morale was perhaps the greater loss. But there was more—she was sunk by a single shell from Germany's latest battleship, *Bismark*. A lucky shot penetrated through to a magazine, which ignited and blew the ship in half. This only served to suggest the superiority of German arms. Churchill demanded that every effort and risk be made and taken to sink the *Bismark*. It was—three days later, with serious loss of life. On the *Hood* it had been worse. Out of a complement of almost 1,500 men there were just three survivors. These were moments that became imprinted on my mind and memory.

We had the usual mixture of one or two outstanding masters, with the majority more or less average. The quality that puts a teacher into the gifted category is the ability to make the subject interesting, to leave his pupils wanting to learn, wanting more. Most had their own idiosyncrasies. One master dealt with any breach of discipline by threatening to have the 'next boy beaten', though seldom did. Our art master, who distinguished himself by always wearing a bow tie, periodically declared he would send any boy that spoke out of turn 'to be flogged', though he never did. He would however go spare if anyone put red and blue next to each other when painting. In his world that was sacrilegious. (I rather *like* red and blue together!) Another was in the habit of throwing chalk at anyone deemed not to be paying the attention he required. One boy—Jim Wotherspoon who figures later in these reminiscences—was on one occasion the recipient of a piece of chalk, which he promptly picked up and threw back at the master! This didn't go down at all well. Not being part of the master's game plan, Jim was promptly marched off to the headmaster for the inevitable caning. Incipient rebellion was to be extinguished at source! I imagine, however, that the Head must have had a quiet word with the master, for the chalk throwing fell into abeyance!

School played a very large part in my life, as it does, I imagine, in every child's life. It was the place where friends and occasional enemies were made. In the shape of homework, it extended into the living room. It was the hub of collective activities, of team games, of camping and suchlike. I met my oldest friend, the same Jim Wotherspoon, on day one at the kindergarten. It is a friendship that endured for almost seventy years until his recent death. It was at school that I discovered my inaptitude for games. If it involves a ball, count me out, the ball will go anywhere but where my intention would have it! Similarly tools—a screwdriver in my hands will at once gain a mind of its own, a mind at complete variance with mine! Mark's comment on one occasion, when I had a tool in my hand and using it in some way—'What is Daddy trying to do?'—has passed into the family archive!

I was nine and a half when war broke out. After bending over backwards to meet the reasonable and unreasonable demands of the German Chancellor, Herr Hitler, the British and French called his bluff, only to discover that he wasn't bluffing. For almost six years a bitter and unforgiving conflict ensued, which, before it ended, had engulfed the larger part of the planet. In the first three years we won hardly anything, the second three we lost hardly anything, finally reducing the Germans to the most total defeat in their history. But not before some fifty million people had paid with their lives. It was an allied victory that owed a vast amount to Russia and the U.S.A. But for a year, with our only ally, the French, beaten, this country faced the German power alone. Hitler with his aggression sowed the wind, and he and his people reaped the whirlwind. The response of us children was just one of excitement. We knew nothing of what hung upon its outcome—only that all sorts of things were happening. Men in khaki or other service uniforms began to appear everywhere. Rationing got underway, and later, as the bombing began, there was more excitement. The first job in the morning after a raid was to rush into the road and hunt for the largest pieces of shrapnel. These would then be taken to school in the hope nobody had anything larger. An anti-aircraft battery was placed about half a mile from our home. The thundering of its guns frequently sounded, which meant the enemy weren't getting it all their own way. In point of fact precious few aircraft were shot down by A.A. guns, but they were effective at boosting morale.

To begin with, as soon as the air raid sirens went, we were hauled out of bed and went across the road to some friends who had had a passage strengthened to form a shelter. This became very tedious, especially on a cold winter's night. This gave way to a place under the stairs which was thought to offer some protection. There came a point when the raids were so frequent that we finished up staying put in bed! We never did have a proper shelter of our own. The nearest we ever came to being bombed, though we were unaware of it at the time, was when our next door neighbours, years later and doing some work in their garden, came across an incendiary bomb that had buried itself!

In 1940, when I was ten, Mr Churchill became prime minister and began speaking from time to time to the British people on the radio, in addition to his speeches to parliament. These have taken their place in the history of this land, peerless examples of the use and power of the English language. About ten minutes before such a speech was to be broadcast, my father would begin to get the radio ready—a heavy, polished wood affair with a fretwork front depicting a sunrise, with the controls on the side. Behind, the back was open, and the several large valves and other machinery could be seen. Switched on, the valves took a couple of minutes to warm up and glowed when they did so. This done, my father fiddled with the knobs until he was satisfied that all was at its best. We then waited. In short order, the announcer would come through first, his precise words forgotten but along these lines: "The Prime Minister, the Right Honourable Mr Winston Churchill, will address the nation." The atmosphere in the room was electric. Not a sound was uttered. And then Mr Churchill spoke—in a style influenced by Gibbon and Tennyson, but which he had made wholly his own. He made clear our position, what was expected of each man and woman; but supremely, he stressed his conviction that we would ultimately prevail. Such was the power underpinning his words that millions across the land took his resolve and made it their own. Some of his words and phrases remain with me still.

Those were memorable times and brave days. Shortages and air raids, rationing and blackouts notwithstanding, it was good to be alive. They put their life-long imprint on this ten-year-old boy. It was well that the prime minister was able to persuade the people that victory would crown their united labours, for no one else in the world believed it. The defeated French generals declared our necks would be wrung in three weeks. The American ambassador to Great Britain, Kennedy (father of the later president) advised the American President Roosevelt that we were finished, and to forget us. Certainly, the odds ranged against us were formidable.

Academically average, at sports and games pretty hopeless, my hobbies were stamp collecting and the piano. This last had to be abandoned on joining my training ship. There was no scope for such refinements on board *H.M.S. Conway*! Though my skill at the keyboard remains very modest, still it proved to be of great value. It quickly became clear that to play any instrument must command absolute attention, never mind the result. In the years that followed it was to be a great solvent of cares and anxieties. An hour at the piano would wash away a day of business worries, at the same time washing away any potential listeners to the furthest extremities of the house! My stamp collection has hardly seen the light of day for over half a century. It could be very time consuming, and time in due course became the most precious commodity of all. Perhaps it ought to he pulled out and checked for items that have become of great rarity and greater worth! Realism, on the other hand, argues that the time required would almost certainly exceed any marketable gain!

One of the joys of wartime was travelling on the Liverpool overhead railway that ran parallel with the dock system, now long gone. Jim, myself and another pal, Peter Irwin, would team up, take a tram to the Pierhead, then onto the overhead, popularly known as 'the dockers' umbrella'. With pencil and pad we would count the number of naval ships—corvettes, destroyers, cruisers, and very occasionally an aircraft carrier or battleship. In addition there would always be large numbers of merchant ships, for Liverpool was the busiest port in the U.K. after London, and as such was a chief target of the Luftwaffe. Afterwards, and as a special treat, a lunch at a department store called the Bon Marche, where, for half a crown (l2.5p) a delicious cold table was on offer. It was self service and as much as wanted could be taken. And much was wanted! The meat section, however, was under the protection of a sharp-eyed supervisor who ensured we took only one slice of one item of meat. And, of the meat, no seconds either! Well, rationing was in force—and it had to be. We made up by piling our plates with vast amounts of the lovely array of tasty salads. The day might he rounded off with a visit to the news theatre where a ticket costing a shilling or one and sixpence (5p–7.5p) gave entry. This allowed you to stay as long as you liked. The collection of film shorts lasted about an hour or a little more. We seldom stayed on after the cycle started again, for not much on offer justified a further viewing.

Peter, one of our little triumvirate (for he, Jim and myself did many things together) left Cowley at thirteen to go to public school. His father had a senior management position and was able to afford the fees. Peter distinguished himself by being a walking travel guide. He knew the least expensive way of getting from anywhere to anywhere! At the cinema he always managed to get to the box office last, in the hope that one of us would have got his ticket for him! We never did! Very sadly he committed suicide in his thirties, putting an end to a promising engineering career.

By the time I was eleven, the idea of a career at sea held me firmly in its grip. Quite why this was so escapes me, for there was no seafaring background on either side of my family. My father had spent a couple of years, wartime only, with the Royal Naval Air Service, but with no thought of making it a permanent occupation. Not surprisingly, my parents didn't take these ideas at all seriously and it took some persuasion to change this.

To forward this aim I asked the headmaster to allow me to drop Latin and replace it with extra maths, a subject of much importance for a naval future. He refused, and when I asked why, seeing it could be of no value for my plans, he declared, "My boy, it makes you think, and that always has value." Not persuaded, but unable to change it, the rebel in me refused to treat the subject as anything other than a waste of time. Not surprisingly, my last Latin exam result was outstanding—outstandingly bad! At 3% it has to be allowed it fell materially below the expectations of the school! Extra maths took over! Everything has its uses, however, and in years to come it was to provide our children with a fire-proof alibi whenever some result was below par. "At least I got 30%, not 3%!" could be counted on as a defence against parental interrogation and criticism! Even grandchildren have been known to call it in aid. Very much later in life I discovered that using the odd Latin word or quote could add colour to a speech or talk!

In the thirties, holidays were still short of being a universal entitlement. From the turn of the century the idea had been gradually gaining ground. Beginning with just single days, various groups little by little negotiated improvements, and many jobs carried a week's paid holiday by the 1930's. My father, because he and his brother ran their own business, was able to take a full fortnight. This was always taken at one go, so it figured as an event of some moment. Their garage business included a taxi service, and the car used for that was the one that took us on holiday. What happened to someone who wanted a taxi during that period was not something that bothered me. Presumably the potential client found someone else.

Packing was the lead in, though I was too young to do much other than get in the way; nonetheless, the frisson of anticipation touched us all, adults no less than children. There was a trunk that seemed to me to be enormous. It had large brass fittings and slats of wood fixed to the outside of the lid and bottom, and which made it look very impressive. What gave it a special presence was that it only came out once a year, and that associated with a very pleasurable coming event. Cars in those days didn't have boots, but my father's had a luggage rack that could he let down at the rear and stuff secured on it. The trunk was always the first item on the rack, followed by lesser cases and sundry items, the whole then firmly tied with rope.

Finally, the day arrived to depart. Our destination might be Devon or Llandudno or some such, never abroad. Always at a guest house or farm, for money was in short supply. Hotels were out of the question. Farms were our favourite; there we could make friends with the animals, learn to milk the cows and go with the milk float to deliver to the customers. The various sorts of milk, full cream, skimmed and so on, were held in large milk churns. The float would have measures with hooked handles that hung at the side—pint, quart, etc. The customers provided their own jugs and the agreed quantity and quality was poured in. It was all great fun and we loved it. All too quickly the two weeks ended and another year had to pass before the next. But a year is so far outside the timescale of a child that it can't reach that far, even in imagination.

One year—I would be about six—our parents began to unpack as soon as we arrived, and I wandered off to check out the lie of the land. To my immense delight there was a large pond and, even better, a small boat and oars. This just had to be tested, and whilst attempting to get on board the boat moved away—in the way that boats do! The end result was that the pond took me in and the boat remained empty. What made for a more interesting result was that the surface of the water was covered with a thick layer of 'jinny green teeth'. My father, responding to cries for help, dragged me out, now covered in the stuff. My mother took over and was less than pleased, for my clothes were among my best. Somehow or other she managed to get me cleaned up without the benefit of bath or shower, for plumbing tended to be limited in these places. The normal provision for ablutions was a large bowl and equally large jug filled with cold water, all placed in the bedroom.

We were brought up by my mother. My father, a figure very much in the background, was easy going and would have spoiled us; he deferred invariably to my mother and never tried to influence her. What she said went. It was pointless trying to lie—she was always ahead of us. A teacher before she married, she gave education a very high priority; school was for academic progress and home for teaching us how to live and behave. Manners were important, as were forms of address. "Do you want?" was unacceptable. Only "Would you like?" would do. When a guest was leaving the house, the door should not be closed until the guest was some little distance away, and then silently. Caps were to be touched whenever meeting with an adult. School reports were scrutinised minutely. The most damning comment was, "Could have done better." My father never read a single school report—he probably took the view his wife studied them sufficiently for them both! Everything gave way to enabling homework to be properly dealt with. In the winter only one fire was lit—in the kitchen. There was no central heating. Only a very small percentage of homes, invariably at the top end of the market, had such luxury. The kitchen was the room with the radio, so my father had to be ready to forego his favourite programme in order that silence should prevail whilst homework was dealt with. He never objected.

Though the car's primary function was to earn its keep as a hire car, until war broke out it was generally available for family use. This gave the impression we were better off than was really the case, for cars were still very much a possession of the minority. The number of families with two cars was miniscule. Though my father was very capable behind a wheel, my mother proved an incorrigible back seat driver. Advice, guidance and instruction poured from her—"Slow down! Not so fast! Watch this! Mind that! Be careful of the oncoming car." Phlegmatically, it all seemed to go over his head. Once, having been urged to slow down several times, he lowered the window and put his hand out. Immediately came the demand: "Norman, *what* are you doing?" Came the reply: "It's all right, there's a woman behind me pushing a pram. I'm just waving her on to overtake me!" It was probably the nearest he ever got to taking exception to being harassed. Despite her enthusiasm for advising others how they should drive, my mother never showed any serious inclination to learn herself.

Whilst my father took life very much as he found it, as long as he had his cigarettes and beer (he was content to let life roll over him), my mother had ambitions. With the passage of time these were increasingly focused on us—that my sister should make a 'good' marriage, and that I should 'get on'. Sent out to shop, my instructions would frequently include, "Now, don't let anyone push you around, let them know who you are!" But, who *was* I? Just one lad among thousands. The thought of carrying out that instruction was just too embarrassing and was never fulfilled. Happily, she never queried whether it had been.

After 1941 few bombs were dropped anywhere in the U.K. Hitler had taken the gamble of his life—a gamble he was to lose. He invaded Russia. Perhaps he should have studied the career of Napoleon a little more closely. He needed all his planes for the Eastern front. This did not stop the allies from steadily increasing their own air attacks on Germany, and they did so right up to the end of the war—by which time vast areas of Germany had been laid waste. In fact, Germany experienced bombing of a ferocity far beyond anything inflicted on this country. So much so, that in the quieter days of peace, some have wondered aloud whether such was justified. But nations that wage unprovoked and aggressive war against peaceful countries, and organise the deliberate, barbaric and cold-blooded murder of seven million people, mustn't be too surprised if they tend to be treated rather roughly in their turn. The raids had been our chief direct involvement in the conflict. Apart from these, the war became a matter of news bulletins and the papers. A broadsheet newspaper was a single sheet, folded in two, to make four pages. Restrictions and shortages we just took in our stride.

From 1942 onwards it became increasingly clear that we were going to win the war. Hitler had attacked Russia, believing he could knock them out in six months, that is, by the end of 1941. He had, after all, beaten the French army in as many weeks, an army thought to be the finest on the continent and which had prevailed in 1918. It was important that he should, for in a protracted conflict, he couldn't begin to command the combined resources of Great Britain, Russia and the U.S.A. As the Russians counter attacked in the winter of 1941, it became clear they were anything but beaten. It was then that the more perceptive Germans realised their war was lost, though it became a capital offence to say so.

For my part, school life continued in the way that school life does. Year by year I put on inches and pounds, ultimately reaching five feet, ten and a half inches, though it wasn't before I turned fifty that I tipped the scales at more than nine stone—this last despite being subjected as a child to several years of a daily spoonful of cod liver oil and malt. Whilst it made no difference whatever, it was thoroughly enjoyable, tasting for all the world like a very soft caramel. Both parents were also lightweights. Taller than my father by a couple of inches, both my sons are taller again at over six feet. Steadily improving diet and health care may probably be responsible for this progression.

Money was in short supply throughout the thirties, and in the forties, though it became easier, there was practically nothing to spend it on. In our family my mother handled all fiscal matters, paid the bills, organised expenditure, and generally oversaw the household economy. My father's contribution was to generate the stuff! She also dealt with all correspondence. A good household manager, she made every shilling (5p) go the distance. Meals were sound but not exciting—the purse didn't allow for much in the way of exotic foods. Game and fowl were almost totally out of reach, a roast chicken was a very rare event, but beef was plentiful and cheap, so that was a staple. Roast on Sunday, it would re-appear in various guises till about the middle of the week, when stews, hotpots and suchlike took over. Sweets centred round rice pudding with occasional sago for variety. Prunes were popular, though not with us! We never visited a restaurant once that I can recall, but occasional meals at a café were not unknown. Department stores often offered catering; I can remember having on one occasion brown Windsor soup and rissoles! Such adventures were sufficiently rare to be memorable.

It was always required that we ate up whatever was put in front of us. If we jibbed, and we sometimes did, the sharp response was always, "There are children all over the world who would be glad to have what you are being given!" (I longed to, but never dared say, "Then let them have it!" The consequences could have been expected to be dire!) There was one vegetable I couldn't, and still can't, handle—Brussels sprouts. Initially required to eat them, they just wouldn't stay down, and there came a point where even my mother recognised, that for me, they were in a class by themselves. From that time on they were not enforced.

On occasion, when taken shopping, a rabbit would be on the agenda. These would be hung outside the butchers or greengrocers in long rows. The customer could select her own, and my mother would prod various ones to try and ensure her choice was suitably plump. Selected, it would be taken into the shop and given to the assistant who would behead it, and strip off the fur. This ritual held my gaze in frozen horror. It was clear to me from an early age that I could never be a surgeon nor yet a butcher. Had I to kill and prepare my own meat, I would undoubtedly become a vegetarian.

From being about eight, possibly seven, pocket money was established at 3d (a little over 1p) a week and remained at that level for several years. This may not sound a lot, but it would buy six ounces of sweets. An inveterate saver, money has never burnt holes in my pockets. Comics didn't have any great appeal, and anyway were much discouraged at home. Sweets, yes, occasionally, but again an eye was kept on how many of those we ate.

Saving came quite naturally to me, though it was invariably linked to a long-term objective, never, absolutely never, as an end in itself. My first purchase of a major item, wholly with my own money, was in 1940 or possibly early 1941. It was an electric table lamp with a shade on which was written an extract from one of Churchill's wartime speeches. It cost 16/11 (85p). Allowing for some contribution from monetary Christmas and birthday presents, that represented about a year's savings. To me therefore it was a major item and considerable time was given to its choice!

TRAINING SHIP

Before reaching my teens, my interest in the sea as a career had crystallised into a firm resolve. At that stage, considering only the Royal Navy, my mother discussed the matter with the headmaster, and arrangements were put in hand for me to sit the scholarship exam for Dartmouth. This could only be taken once, so at the age of twelve I was ushered into a room on my own, to make what I could of the several exam papers. In the event, the result suggested not a lot, for in due time a letter arrived to say I had failed. Had I known before sitting that only twelve scholarships a year were made available for the whole country, it might have dissuaded me from proceeding. That I might have been among the brightest twelve, even with all the optimism of youth, was a hope or ambition beyond my grasp. The exam couldn't he taken again, and even if it could, the same result would certainly have obtained. That door was closed, permanently.

Twelve is not a good age at which to come to terms with one's inadequacies, although it must be allowed that life subsequently enabled, through frequent practice, a more philosophical approach to such matters. The question was, where now? Unwilling to abandon my hopes entirely, these shifted from the R.N. to the M.N. In the event it made much sense, for in those days a commission in the R.N. would not have been easy to sustain without a private income, and of that there was no chance whatever.

There were three possibilities—Panghourne Naval College, *H.M.S. Worcester*, or *H.M.S. Conway*. All took youngsters who wanted to train for the merchant navy, and also a smaller number for the Royal Navy. Their application age was later, from fourteen onwards, so another year plus was spent at Cowley until, once again, I was ushered into a room to sit exams—this time for *H.M.S. Conway*. My parents had decided they would bite the bullet and pay for me, so it was not wholly surprising that this time my labours appeared to meet with approval, and I was to start with the September 1944 term. The war had helped the business to become a little more profitable than in the barren thirties, but it must still have been a difficult decision for them to take. School fees at Cowley had been £10 a year, whereas on the *Conway* they were £250—a huge increase, and one that wasn't easily accommodated. Mercifully, it was only for two years. The reason *Conway* was chosen was in part because it was based on the river Mersey, though temporarily (so it was thought at the time) moved to the Menai Straits; because it had been local, my father knew one or two who had links with the ship. Even in Wales it was still also the nearest, and had a reputation at least the equal of the other two. It had produced its fair share of admirals with an odd air marshal or two, though its most famous son was the poet and writer John Masefield.

So it was that, at fourteen years and four months, I found myself sitting upright on a gritty, steam powered L.M.S. train, and with my parents, heading for Bangor in North Wales. Third class on the London Midland and Scottish service had seating which encouraged one to be upright!

Sometime previous to this date with destiny, instructions had been received to proceed to the Liverpool Sailors Home in Paradise Street, Liverpool. A perfect example of how completely streets can be misnamed! It proved to be a gaunt building which, like all others of the period, was heavily encrusted with grime and soot, a by-product of a multitude of smoking chimneys. It reared gracelessly to a height of half a dozen or more stories. Once inside, every floor had a type of cloister, off which led the various rooms. In the centre was an atrium that rose to the topmost height of the building. This might have been rather striking had it not been for the wire netting that was stretched across the open space at each floor level. Apparently several suicides had taken place, encouraged by the ease with which a man could jump over the handrail from an upper balcony. The optimism of youth prevented my wondering why they might wish to take such drastic action.

Arriving at the room dedicated to fitting out *Conway* cadets with their uniforms, we—my mother was with me—were greeted by the manager and his assistant. This latter, a man of indeterminate years who was never quite drunk and never quite sober, was left to take all the measurements, it being rather beneath the dignity of one as senior as the manager to perform this task. This clearly suited the junior, for he seemed to find a job satisfaction in the measuring bit somewhat beyond the purely professional. A vigilant parent ensured there was no overt extension of these tasks. The measurements duly noted, I was free to study a glass case in which were forty or fifty cap badges of all the shipping companies that took *Conway* cadets on completion of their training. It was a captivating sight of gold and silver wire and coloured emblems, fashioned into a medley of insignia. In the way of these things, some of the largest and most impressive belonged to the least satisfactory companies. This was hidden from me at the time.

Paperwork completed and signatures obtained, we returned home to await delivery. An exciting moment, for everything was exactly as ordered, including the peaked cap and badge. This last was R.N., an anchor on a red velvet cushion under the royal crown, and surrounded by gold wire fashioned into a fernlike border. Boys on the ship were given the honorary rank of cadet R.N.R. The cap was complete with a stiffener, a wire that fitted round the inside of the perimeter, the presence of which unfailingly identified one on board as a 'New Chum', the label given to first term boys. One of the earliest things to be done on settling down on the ship was to remove this very visible give away, and jump on the cap a few times to try and give it a well worn look! Becoming a seasoned old salt was a high priority!

Conway was anchored in the Menai Straits, a few hundred yards from Bangor Pier on one side, and the Gazelle Slip on the Anglesey side. Unlike the *Victory*, which she very much resembled, she still floated and turned to the tide. As such she was the last of the old wooden walls of the British navy to do so. It was, in part, the reason why, when the heavy bombing of Liverpool began, she was moved to safer waters.

When first built, *Conway* was a second rate ship of the line. The rating of a ship owed nothing to better or worse, only to the number of guns carried. *Victory*, a first rate, had a hundred and eight, while *Conway* had ninety-two. Commissioned in 1839 as *H.M.S. Nile*, her keel had been laid no less than twelve years earlier in 1827. The nation was not at war with any other major country at the time, and there was no urgency for more battleships. Indeed, by the time she was completed she was virtually obsolete, and an attempt was made to bring her into the dawning steam age by fitting auxiliary steam engines that drove a screw propeller. Smoke escaped through a demountable funnel, stored out of the way when not in use. Quite what the smoke did to the sails and shrouds can best be imagined. The grit and filth that must have poured out of the funnel when the engines below were operating would hardly have endeared this modern invention to the deck hands.

Commissioned for a voyage, the full complement was eight hundred and fifty men, to which must he added stores for up to three months, including water, together with ammunition to feed the guns. Living conditions on board must have been appalling. By comparison, as a training ship she was considered full with two hundred and fifty cadets, plus a handful of executive officers and working hands. And fresh water was being brought off daily from the shore, as were provisions. The guns had been removed and no ammunition was needed, both of which had taken up a large amount of space. Despite all this, cadets had only the area taken by their sea chest and a slung hammock to call their own. No wonder they had to resort to press gangs to get men to serve, and even those languishing in the dreadful jails of the time, sometimes refused the offer of their freedom in exchange for serving on a naval ship. Often navy ships had to sail without their full complement. Sufficient men just couldn't be found.

Soon after we arrived at the pier a motorboat manned by cadets came across to take us to the ship. Bowman, sternman, engineer and cox made up her complement. This last was effectively the 'captain'. All looked to me big, strong and supremely confident of their boating skills. I began to feel rather small and inadequate (5'1" in my socks!) and wondered whether I'd ever be able to handle a boat with such skill and panache as they. Perhaps this is the moment to note that on the day I joined the ship I was just fourteen and four months; the average age of my peers was about fifteen and a half.

Looking back, it is hard to realise just how vast the gulf can be between fourteen and fifteen. My voice hadn't broken and it was to be a few months before it did, a condition that resulted in contumely being heaped upon me. At the time this seemed to me very unreasonable—after all, I was not responsible for when my voice broke. Such logic, however, reckoned without the downside impact on others. If a boy still with his treble was thought able to handle the training, this would do nothing to support the important image of the tough, hard tack, seaman—an image that was important to quite a number.

In little time, and preceded by a flurry of orders from the cox, the boat arrived flawlessly alongside the gangway that led to the lower deck. A bugler, cadet captain and the officer of the watch hovered. They were polite to my parents whilst managing more or less to ignore me. There was a general sense of hustle, of activity, of people on the move, all interspersed periodically by bugle calls, all of which had specific meanings but which were lost on me completely. These were the calls new chums were expected to master within a fortnight. It was round about this point that I wondered what madness had led me to this moment, to these sounds and smells and activity, to all of which I was an utter stranger and knew not a soul.

Somebody, probably the cadet captain, pointed us to the gangway that led to the orlop deck below. This was the deck where a couple of square feet were taken up by a sea chest on which was painted my name, complete with initials. Most cadets had their accommodation on this deck, though accommodation was a fairly generous term, for it consisted of the sea chest and space to sling a hammock. There were some cupboards let into the side of the ship for storing school gear such as exercise books and the like. These weren't very popular because the rats were able to get into them and they had developed a taste for the glue that was used to bind the spines. Still they were used, because alternatives were just not available.

Of the group joining the ship when I did, one boy's parents asked that he be shown to his cabin. With a disbelieving smile, the officer of the watch explained that cadets didn't have cabins, but that chest and hammock were supplied—whereupon both boy and parents returned ashore to be seen no more. No great encouragement was given to parents to hang about, so after a fairly cursory look around, leave was taken. Previously, I had made it indelibly clear that under no circumstances was my mother to attempt to kiss me on departing! Thus, having shaken hands with both, they embarked for the shore. In retrospect, shaking hands with one's mother must have seemed a great deal more surprising than kissing her! It appeared otherwise to me at the time.

I was now free to contemplate my new home, holidays excluded, for the next two years. It was not very reassuring. All my peers were bigger and stronger, a disparity perhaps largely accounted for by the age difference. Boys can routinely grow two or more inches in a year. It could be the difference between a broken and a treble voice and for me it certainly was. Then there was the movement—everyone seemed to be coming or going. Bugle calls interspersed everything, many of which were summons to some form of action by one group or another. Perhaps it was well therefore that we were given little time to dwell on such matters, for the senior cadet captain of the top to which we were assigned, called us together and began the task of instructing us in the ways of the ship. Like most senior c.c.'s. it was his last term, at the end of which he would be joining the shipping company of his choice, and so the beginning of his career proper.

Cadet captains, junior, senior and headed by a chief cadet captain, were the backbone of the day-to-day operation of the ship. They answered to a small team of executive officers, in addition to whom there was a full time chaplain. They were all under the overall command of the captain and all lived on board. Cadets were divided into 'tops,' with names that reflected the part of the ship in which they lived, such as 'quarterdeck', 'port mizzen', 'starboard main', etc. Responsible for the conduct and operational performance of each top was a senior and junior cadet captain. Included in the duties of each top was the task of maintaining the cleanliness of a defined section of the ship. All cadets learned the rudiments of martial drill. Perfected by regular practice, *Conway* boys could put on a brave show, led by their own bugle and drum band.

There were also a number of supernumerary c.c's. who were charged with looking after such as the boats. These were popular berths, for it gave opportunity to spend rather more time ashore than would otherwise obtain. The 'water boat' was most sought after of all, for it took over an hour to fill and gave time for the crew to have a smoke (strictly forbidden) in relative safety, and perhaps a walk into town. This boat was really a large floating tank whose chief use was ferrying fresh water to the ship. It also came in handy for transporting largish numbers of people, being able to accommodate more than any of the other boats.

Much depended on the way a c.c. discharged his office, and his powers were considerable. The executive officers invariably sought to back up their c.c.'s, knowing how much of the orderly running of the ship depended on them. Those who had a tendency to authoritarianism could make life disagreeable, but this was the exception. They also needed to remember that at the end of term their authority evaporated. There was one occasion when a c.c. who had made himself rather disliked by his peers, at the end of term found he was quite badly roughed up by those who believed he had mistreated them. There was not a lot the officers could do, as all those involved were leaving the ship for good.

To enforce his will, the c.c. had a number of sanctions at his disposal. Pumping the bilges was both a well used, and a necessary one. The ship, wholly of wooden construction, was copper sheathed below the water line, but still was leaking quite steadily, requiring daily pumping of the bilges. This translated into many minor breaches being rewarded with a couple of hundred strokes of the pump, whose chief accessory was a long iron handle, and which consumed significant energy in its operation.

Then there was 'slack party'. There were always jobs that needed doing but which were unattractive, if not positively disagreeable, and for which volunteers would be thin on the ground. The most onerous was 'the coal hole'. Coal to fire the boiler was stored in the bowels of the ship, and quantities had to he lifted periodically to a point adjacent to meet its needs. This required those in the coal storage to fill the containers and others to operate the hoist and empty the buckets. It was dirty work. Those on slack party were given so many hours of such work to be performed in their free time. The one consolation was a bath at the end!

Many punishments therefore were very practical in their design, and could be considered positive or creative. The most common of all, though, was the corporal use of a rope's end. Nicknamed a 'teaser', it consisted of about a yard of rope whipped at one end and sometimes with a loop spliced into the other end. The more sadistic soaked the business end in brine to stiffen it. Used with vigour, it caused a sharp pain, but which subsided quite quickly. Apprehension was probably the worst part. Normally, little, if any, ill feeling was engendered by its use, and the custom was for hands to be shaken immediately afterwards. Occasionally, the miscreant would be offered alternative punishments. I can recall no occasion when other than the rope's end was chosen. All these methods of enforcing the will of authority were made clear to us at our induction, together with at least some of the breaches that would activate them.

One of the first things to he learnt was the slinging and subsequent lashing up and stowing of our hammocks, for we should be sleeping in one that night. Each cadet was given his own and it was his responsibility to ensure it was in good order. There was a rope used for slinging, and another for lashing it after use. This last involved ensuring that the blankets, pillows, etc., were under the overlapping canvas sides. The rope was then used to make seven half hitches round the whole length, rather as a long piece of beef might he tied. The testing moment for us new chums was the c.c. taking the finished product and bending it vigorously. Any slackness and the blankets and sheets would become exposed following this treatment. Should this happen, the luckless owner could expect one stroke of the teaser for each scrap made visible!

Whilst expected to master the bugle calls within the first two weeks, not many succeeded, and there were many surreptitious efforts to check what some of the less frequently used ones meant. One, however, was learnt very speedily. It was distinctive, but even had it not been, the primitive urge of hunger would have ensured rapid understanding. It was the call to the mess deck for the next meal! Meals were taken on the main deck, which with a little ingenuity served also as the classroom deck, and also functioned as the chapel, providing the setting for Sunday divisions. It was there that the organ was installed.

Hunger was universal and continuous. The Second World War was in its later stages and very strict rationing was in force. Two hundred and fifty teenage boys leading very active lives would have tested any catering organisation, even in normal times. In stringent wartime conditions it must have been a nightmare. Even bread was rationed. The food could hardly be described as appetising, but it must have been adequate, for we all grew apace, and for my own part I put on pounds and inches. Supplies from the shore came aboard daily, many in large wicker hampers, and these were attacked frequently by those doing the transporting. To counter this they were fitted with strong locks, and for a time this resolved the 'shrinkage'. Then came the day when authority discovered that the lid hinges had been unscrewed and food again taken!

My own outstanding memories relating to food include a pot of jam which, when opened, had nestling in the top a small collection of worms that were, no doubt, thoroughly enjoying their nourishing surroundings! Once (or was it twice?) each term we were given a one-pound pot of jam to be used as we saw fit. Guarding it safely between uses in our lockable sea chests was essential. On discovering the livestock, my first reaction was to report it to the duty officer. He took one look at it, said "Scrape them off!" in a tone that suggested I lacked all initiative, dismissed me, and got on with the rest of his life! Jam being one of the more valuable of one's assets, I did just that. The thought of losing a whole pot of jam would have been a disaster too great.

My first Friday lunch on board was a different matter. Because some cadets were Roman Catholic, fish was always served on Fridays. This particular Friday it was battered cod and boiled potatoes. On cutting through the batter, the first thing I saw were two dead cockroaches. That put paid to my lunch, hungry or not! It was the last time I could contemplate battered cod on the ship, and indeed for some time afterwards. Perhaps what made it worse was the fact that I had only been on the ship for about four days and was still very homesick. In retrospect, that was the moment of touching bottom, and I left the mess deck wondering why on earth I had got myself into this strange and forbidding world. Homesickness passed, and by the end of the first week I had come to terms with my new life, and determined to try and make something of it.

Cadets in their second year stood night watch, for there was never a moment when the ship was without its eyes and ears. A popular haunt between rounds was the galley where a good strong cup of cocoa could he brewed. This warm retreat was shared with a numerous contingent of rats that welcomed its attractions no less than us. A solid piece of wood that formed a handy club was part of the standard equipment and was used regularly to have a go at any of the beasts that came within reach.

On one occasion when on watch, and repairing to the galley, it was clear we were going to have baked beans for breakfast, for there was a large cauldron of the stuff on top of an oven. This was not an infrequent dish, often alternating with scrambled egg made from egg powder (one of the war's less attractive inventions). Its distinctive characteristic was a greenish colour at the edges when served in a metal dish. In this collection of beans was a half submerged, dead rodent. Either it had slipped when running along an overhead pipe, or been knocked off by an earlier enterprising watchkeeper. It was more than I was willing to do to fish it out, but no doubt one of the galley staff arriving in the morning did just that, for baked beans were served as usual. How many times did this sort of thing go on behind the scenes? Who knows? A case perhaps of 'what the eye doesn't see, the heart…' This eye having seen, though, did put a slightly different perspective on the matter, and I forewent my share of beans that morning. Last word: no one seemed the slightest bit the worse for wear following their beans. Maybe it really is all in the mind!

Life on board was fairly intensively organised, free time very limited and therefore much prized. It was also designed to be physically demanding, in large part for its own sake and value, but was also thought by cadets, in conjunction with bromide laced coffee, to be the authorities' answer to the burgeoning sexuality of a bunch of healthy teenagers. The evidence that it worked was not persuasive. Whether there is anything betwixt heaven and earth that would so work must be thought extremely doubtful. Reveille was at 6-30 a.m. with a loud and unwelcome bugle call and the officer of the watch walking the deck shouting, "Rise and shine, show a leg!" Response tended to be prompt, despite the desire to spend just a little longer within the delicious comfort of a hammock, for one disadvantage of a hammock is that it is particularly easy to tip a body out of—an exercise some c.c.'s were not unwilling to indulge. Even though slung less than two feet from the deck, landing unceremoniously on the hard oak wood was not the best way to begin the day. But there was another compelling reason for not delaying—ablutions!

Right forward on the lower deck were the washbasins, probably about fifty or so, each equipped with one tap—a cold tap. But there were five times that number of cadets. New chums, unless they had actually got a bowl and were washing, could be displaced by any hand senior to them. This meant they would be the last to get their turn. Summer or winter, it was all the same—only cold water was available, *if* it was available at all. The basins were all served from an adjacent storage tank by means of a single pipe. This was of a bore that couldn't begin to serve all the basins at once. New chums were invariably relegated to those furthest from the tank, so when they opened the tap nothing happened. The more enterprising bent down, got their mouths round it, and started to suck vigorously until a little water began to be drawn their way. With luck, a few inches would trickle into the bowl before some other enterprising soul further down the line, likewise sucking for all he was worth, would draw the supply away.

There was little to persuade anyone to linger once the job was done, for being right forward there were two large openings through which the anchor ropes were rove. The wind could be piercing, especially in winter, encouraging a rapid completion. It was fortunate that few had to shave more than once a week, for there was no provision for any hot water. Those who had reached the stage of shaving could wait until it was their turn for the weekly bath, and where hot water was available.

There were only a small number of baths, which meant that they had to be used on a fairly continuous basis. The result was that each cadet got one per week, special factors, like coaling, apart. Each had to clean his bath after use, and this was rather tiresome as the glaze had long since been rubbed off, and the dirt able therefore to get well dug in. It could take as long as the bath itself, and had to be done to the satisfaction of the fellow in charge. The wealthy could invariably find some impecunious cadet to do the job for them. The going rate was sixpence (2.5p).

Dressing took moments only, the distinctive bit being the dark blue shirt, white being reserved for Sunday. The blue colour was chosen because it had to last for six days and didn't show the dirt! At least we didn't have to do our own laundry—this was taken ashore somewhere every week.

Each weekday before breakfast, there was P.T. This ranged from conventional exercises to climbing the rigging. The first time of embarking on this last was heart stopping. The mainmast from the deck to the truck at the very top was about ninety feet (as a commissioned ship of the line, it would have been closer to a hundred and thirty feet). About half way up was a platform that projected several feet on all sides from the mast. From the deck to this halfway point standing rigging supported the mast. Between the stays ratlines ran horizontally, forming footholds for climbing. The closer the stays came to the mast, the narrower the gap bridged by the ratlines and the more difficult to get a proper foothold. Shortly before reaching the platform were the futtocks. These were further stays between the outer edge of the platform and again the mast. They too were equipped with ratlines. The climber had to transfer himself to these as best he could and ascend the short distance of some seven or eight feet whilst hanging backwards at an angle of about forty-five degrees and some forty or so feet above the deck. Making progress, the next stage was to pull oneself around the edge of the platform to get a grip of the next upward set of stays, similar to the first. These ended at a point several feet below the very top of the mast.

The object from here was to move over to the other side of the mast, ready to begin the descent. Footholds were rather precarious, the ratlines having ended some way further down, and there was little to offer much security. It became easier as the descent proceeded; the stays widened enough to allow the ratlines to reappear, but then the fearsome futtocks had to be negotiated again, this time in reverse. Now one had to let the lower half of the body drop over the edge, and then swing it until legs and feet made contact with the stays receding beneath at the same forty-five degree angle. With feet in secure contact with a ratline, the key was to lower the rest of one's body over, little by little, until completely on the futtock stays, once again hanging backwards at a forty-five degree angle over the deck below. The transfer from the bottom end of the futtock back to the lower set of stays was relatively easy, and descent from there was a pretty straight-forward climb down back to the deck. With regular practice fear faded, and it became a matter of some pride to be among the fastest to complete the exercise. But that first time, most cadets will remember for the rest of their lives.

Breakfast followed with most ready to eat just about anything that was on offer. At each mess table (these doubled as desks later on) a cadet captain sat at the head with the members of his top ranged down either side. The table was laid with an oilcloth, shiny on top and, save for a short period after renewal, black-ened and soiled underneath. One cadet was detailed to collect the food, which tended to be such as the gourmet dishes touched on above—baked beans and green-edged scrambled egg. Sometimes there were limited amounts of seconds available. This was the signal for an almighty rush by the duty cadet of each mess to get to the galley in time. The cadet that failed to make it before the supply ran out could expect to receive a rather hostile welcome from his peers on returning empty handed.

To the main dish was added bread and a miniscule sliver of butter, or some-thing that masqueraded as butter. This last was delivered to the mess as a small slab, which was passed to the c.c. who then traced lines along the top, dividing it into the requisite number of pieces. Having taken the first piece himself, which generally managed to be a bit larger than the rest, the slab was passed down the line, each cutting his bit as indicated by the lines. The chap at the end would be lucky if his hadn't suffered from 'shrinkage'. Tea washed all these delicacies down and fortified us for what lay ahead, but not before one further ritual.

Once all the plates etc. had been removed, the oilcloth had to be wiped. Beginning at the c.c.'s end, each cadet wiped his bit and passed the cleaning cloth on. A clean dishcloth was supplied each week, but by the end of the first day, hav-ing collected everything from porridge remains to blobs of gravy, it was a sorry sight. Before the end of the week it had become utterly vile, horrible to hold, ran-cid and evil smelling. But there was no escaping the progress of the thing to one's own patch, when it had to be grabbed and dealt with.

The quickest way to achieve instant popularity, though usually of limited duration, was to he the recipient of a food parcel. These tended not to be fre-quent, if only because the donors were subject to the same rationing as the rest of us. The very infrequency perhaps added to the boundless pleasure when such manna did finally surface. Gathered like bears round a honey pot, the cry would rise from a dozen voices: "Any spare, chum?" Never in the field of human relationships were so many friends made, in so short a time for so plain a purpose!

Maintopmen excepted, all other cadets had to clear off the main deck as quickly as possible, to let those seasoned old salts get on with the job of setting up the classrooms. The mess tables and benches were re-arranged appropriately, and partitions that had been hooked onto the deck head were lowered, and behold, six or eight classrooms were immediately brought into being, whilst blackboards emerged from some storage point. By this time masters had been brought off from the shore and were ready to take up their allotted places. It was important for them to be able to teach without shouting or raising their voices too much, for soundproof the partitions were not. Just one loud voice would carry the length of the deck, partitions or not.

Probably very few joined *Conway* in order to excel academically. Classical subjects were dropped, and their place taken by nautical subjects such as navigation, seamanship, signals, and ship construction. At best the standard might be thought average. At the end of the two-year course, a certificate could be gained that was claimed to be the equal of the then nationally recognised 'School Certificate'. Perhaps it was. The teaching of life skills was another matter. There were few who left that ship unable to hold their own and stand on their own two feet, or as the jargon had it, "One hand for yourself and the other for the ship."

In short order, all traces of food and eating being removed and classrooms created, we assembled for the morning lessons. Like any other teaching establishment, those charged with our enlightenment ranged from the excellent to the barely adequate. The headmaster had been called up and the second master, a man called Carter (his universally used nickname was 'Bogbrush' and owed its origin to a hairstyle which was eerily reminiscent of that implement) was in overall charge for the duration. My chief recollection is that he was ambidextrous, the chalk moving easily from one hand to the other with no obvious difference in the result. Even in those far off days there can have been few teachers who were called on to impart their wisdom in more trying circumstances. In a period of overfull employment they could undoubtedly have found more convenient berths. Perhaps it was the very singular circumstances that were the attraction, and appealed to those who wanted something a little different. Whatever the reason, it wasn't given to us to question their motives.

One man commanded the respect of every boy on the ship—J.D.Weir. He taught navigation, and prior to his joining *Conway* had been chief officer of an oil tanker that had been sunk by a U-Boat. He had been subject to the most horrific burns, his face deeply scarred, ears burnt to stumps, the rest of his body no doubt, similarly affected. His posting to us was a form of advanced convalescence. He had a very gentle and kindly disposition that may, in part at least, have grown out of those terrible experiences. There was among us a silent awareness of what he must have endured, and perhaps a dawning understanding of what could be the price of seafaring in wartime.

Somehow or another, despite the unpromising environment, we absorbed sufficient knowledge to ensure that we would be acceptable to the shipping companies we wished to join. The Captain, Tom Goddard, towards the end of each term, spoke to us at Sunday divisions. He stressed the importance of good results if he was to secure us our places with the best companies. By the end of the first year we could have given his speech for him—it changed by hardly a syllable! Little weight was attached to his urgings for it was widely understood that with the heavy losses of officers and men in the merchant navy, there was a very strong and continuing demand for new blood. And we were the blood that was new.

Sport played a material role in the ship's curriculum, though not in mine personally, for sport in all its manifestations passed me by—and sixty years later continues to do so! One of my more rewarding discoveries was to find that those who showed little aptitude were relegated to something called 'cheering party'. It was not difficult to demonstrate to all appropriate bodies my want of skill in anything that involved a ball, the size, composition and shape of which made little difference. From this point on my contribution to the substantial success the ship enjoyed in competitive sports was to cheer as lustily as required. This, I found, could be combined quite conveniently with reading a book. The two activities are not at all mutually exclusive.

Because the ship had been moved quite hurriedly to avoid the bombing, arrangements for shore-based games were less than ideal. For most, it involved a couple of miles walk to Beaumaris (buses cost money which could otherwise he spent on food) where arrangements had been made to use a sometime prison as a changing room. Executions had been carried out there, which aroused our slightly macabre interest. After the game, there was another walk back. Probably the authorities were quite pleased at the additional energy that would have been consumed getting to the playing fields and back.

For some strange reason I enjoyed cross-country running. These were not overly long, perhaps five or six miles. A telling reason may well have been that as a lightweight I enjoyed an advantage, having less to carry round, and therefore tended to be somewhere near the front.

The other sport, which did capture me, was swimming. Our 'pool' was the Menai Straits, and on days when swimming was ordained, boats would be detailed off to patrol the area as a safety measure. The decision to swim was the warrant officer's, and the rule was that the water had to be 60°F or more. And that could seem quite cold, despite our youth. However, if the thermometer failed to register the right temperature, and the officer had nevertheless predetermined that swim we would, he simply breathed on the bulb until it reached the required sixty, whereupon it would be, "Right lads, in you go!" In practice therefore we could find ourselves in water hardly more than about 55°F! My recollection of diving (there was no other way save jumping) was of finding it almost impossible to breathe for what seemed ages—in practice no doubt only seconds. Breath recovered, swimming of a very vigorous order was encouraged! During the summer months we tended to have large numbers of jellyfish for company. They must have been a harmless variety for I have no recollection of anyone being stung. There were brave souls, though never of their company, who dived in from great heights such as the upper deck, and which must have been thirty or more feet above sea level. Very properly, they appeared heroes in our eyes.

Come Sunday, life moved down a notch. We were allowed to sleep in until 7-00 a.m., a greatly valued concession. If my memory serves, there was no P.T. that day, and some slight attempt was made to make the meals more attractive. The central feature was church parade, followed by a church service. Dressed in white shirts and our best uniforms, we lined up in proper order to be inspected by the captain, also dressed in his best. The difference was that he was awash with gold and medal ribbons. Four gold bands on each sleeve, and gold oak leaves on his cap, made for a very impressive ensemble. For this ceremony he emerged from his home aft where he lived with his wife and daughter in, what seemed to us, unimaginably spacious splendour. In the way of these things the daughter married an old *Conway*—one Fraser, who played a particularly demanding part in the war manning miniature submarines. His bravery won him the Victoria Cross, and, unlike many, he has lived to wear it.

Sunday divisions completed, a church service followed, led by the resident chaplain, a Rev T. Vickery. Appropriately young, he had a strong sporting bent and was the fastest short distance runner on the ship. His time for the hundred yards was beyond the reach of any cadet during my two years. Needless to say, he didn't appear young to us, for he must have been in his later twenties. He found achieving the balance between upholding authority on the one hand, and winning the confidence of the cadets on the other, difficult. From the viewpoint of us cadets he never succeeded, for he was perceived as a pillar of authority. Lamentably, though probably not surprisingly, I cannot recall a single word of any of his sermons.

In my second term the cadet organist left. There was need of a replacement. It was the ship's grievous misfortune to get me. Having spent a few years learning the piano, I was pounced on. If there were others who had learnt similarly, they were keeping their heads down. So me it had to be, though I had never so much as sat in front of an organ before, let alone tried to play one. Not surprisingly, the results were pretty desperate. The chaplain put a brave face on it, and quietly encouraged me. He must have prayed for a more promising student to emerge, though his prayers were unheard, or if heard, then completely disregarded. In the event they were stuck with me for the rest of my time on board. Over a period, people just resigned themselves to their fate.

Sunday was a day of more free time than any other. Letters were usually written, some would read, while others might try and get up to speed on some schoolwork. On a fine day numbers might he found strolling and chatting on the upper deck. Indoor games were often organised in the hold. The hold was also the place where the weekly cinema show was held. There was only one projector, so everything went into an extended pause whilst the cadet operator changed the reels. If he took longer than was thought necessary, he would be noisily urged to greater endeavours. Invariably a song would be sung whilst waiting, generally more or less ribald in character. Authority, wisely, never attempted to intervene. 'Roll me Over' was popular as was 'Coming round the Mountain', though in both cases some verses experienced modification!

Even at the youthful age of fourteen, I had firm and clear religious convictions—not an unalloyed asset on a training ship. Before turning in at night, a bugle call sounded for 'prayers', and during this two minute spell there was an unaccustomed quiet across the decks. Cadets tidied their clothes, whispered to their friends, or made last minute adjustments to their hammocks. What didn't happen was that anyone actually prayed! My first night all was so strange that the two minutes were up before I had collected my thoughts properly.

Throughout the next day, and between bouts of homesickness, I wrestled with what was going to be a challenge. When the bugle for prayer was sounded, it was 'now or never'. In fear and trepidation I sank to my knees by the side of my hammock, aware, from observation the previous night, that I should be alone in a very visible exercise. It remains a most demanding moment in my life. There was some disparagement, and others distanced themselves from such an oddity lest they should be compromised, but there was also some positive response, though offered covertly. Quickly, though, in the way of these things, it became accepted that I was a trifle strange, and life moved on!

Boat work formed a basic part of our training, greatly helped by the fact we were anchored offshore. This created endless opportunity for practice, as stores and supplies of all sorts, including water and coal, were brought from Bangor. There was a considerable movement of people to and from the ship every day as well. Cadets manned all the boats, both powered and oared. There were a number of sailing dinghies and these too were extensively used. There were three motorboats, one of which was the already mentioned water boat. The other two were general purpose, named, not very imaginatively, No.1 and No.2. Again it was a popular role to be appointed to either. Rowing was practiced in the two ten oared cutters and one twelve oared. We all became proficient oarsmen for they were in almost continual use. The two ten oared boats were used for competitions between tops. Finally, there was the captain's gig, a handsome long and narrow boat. Half a dozen of the best oarsmen manned her for the mainly ceremonial occasions on which she was used, such as bringing off the admiral who had been persuaded to give the prizes on speech day.

My chief recollection of rowing was right at the beginning of my first term. It was my first time holding an oar. At the time I was just 5'1" and a little over six stone in weight. From the outset the oar seemed huge to me, very long and heavy; but with difficulty I managed not to 'catch any crabs' (that is, get out of sync with the other oars and so clash with them). As we headed back to the gangway, the order was given, "Toss oars!" I tried my level best, but just hadn't got the strength to lift mine to the vertical position required. The result was an unseemly crash as the oar banged into the side of the ship and ruined the coxswain's otherwise immaculate manoeuvre. He was not, understandably, best pleased with my efforts, but probably realised the problem. From that time on my position was in the bows, where the narrowing of the boat meant the oars were much smaller and lighter. Those were manageable.

Being bowman meant jumping ashore or onto a slipway with a rope just as the boat was coming alongside, put the rope through a ring and so tie the forward end. On one occasion, when our destination was the Gazelle slipway on Anglesey, I jumped as usual but missed my footing and landed in the water just as the cutter came alongside. The cox could do nothing to stop the boat and a few crushed ribs resulted. The up side of this was some days in Bryn Mel, the ship's shore side infirmary. The food there was immeasurably better than on board—well worth a few squashed, but unbroken ribs!

In the evening, all the boats not required were hoisted out of the water on standing davits. This was done manually by cadets pulling on twin sets of rope that lifted the fore and aft ends of the boat. Once at the right height, a cadet detailed to each fall had a short length of lighter rope called a 'stopper', which he wrapped round it. This done, other cadets very quickly tied the fall round a cleat, the stopper then being unwound. For them to have enough free rope to do this required that at the order 'lay to', all those who had been hauling, flung their bit forward vigorously, so creating enough loose rope for the cleat. A popular trick played on new chums was for the chap behind one such, to whisper in a helpful and friendly manner, that on the order 'lay to' he should pull with all his might. Two dozen burly fellows flinging the rope forward and one poor new chum heaving on it, simply meant that he went crashing into his peers amid fearsome imprecations, threats of dire retribution, and a few punches! New chums quickly learnt to treat unauthorized advice with caution.

Aft on the lower deck was the sick bay, where a nursing sister held sway. She lived on board and had her quarters adjacent to the bay. She herself was always spotlessly turned out in a smart white nurse's uniform, complete with headgear. She looked the part and inspired confidence, whilst her seat of operations looked and smelt very clean. Coughs and colds were all that the majority of us ever suffered from. Such were quickly despatched with a few drops or a spoonful of cough medicine. No doubt aided by long experience, she could spot a malingerer at fifty paces, and few were good enough actors to get past her. There were a couple of beds in the bay, but anything infectious was rapidly sent off to Bryn Mel. For the most part we enjoyed rude health.

Lavish supplies of pocket money were strongly discouraged, the advised amount being one shilling a week (5p) with a further small sum for stamps, etc. Anything above 1/6 (7.5p) was frowned on. But costs were correspondingly low. A bottle of O.K. sauce was 4d (1.5p). One bottle would flavour a large quantity of bread! Buns could be bought in the canteen for about half a p. Almost all pocket money went on food, where volume rather than delicacy was the determining factor. The canteen opened at specific times and was indicated by a bugle call. This produced a rush which for new chums was invariably in vain, for unless actually being served when a more senior man arrived, the senior would push him back. It frequently happened that from being almost at the front, he would finish behind scores of his more senior fellows. The payoff was in succeeding terms, when he would unhesitatingly do the same to his juniors!

At sunset, the last post was always played as the flag was lowered at the stern; cadets stopped whatever they were doing, turned to face it, and stood to attention. Well played, it is a haunting tune of which we never tired. There was a vigorous bugle and drum band, and it always fell to the best bugler on the ship to play the last post. It had been in my mind to try and become a bandsman. Anyone could volunteer. That, however, was before I had tried to master the bugle. It is a ferociously difficult thing to get any meaningful sound out of at all—certainly it defeated me. My enthusiasm for the band receded.

In the fourth term (the course was six terms) all cadets spent a month at the Outward Bound Sea School at Aberdovey. This was the first of what were to become a group of such places. It was very popular, not least because the food was so much better. The idea had originated with the Alfred Holt Shipping Co. They subsidised the cost. The idea was to bring together lads from a wide spectrum of social backgrounds, produce a character-building environment, and bridge the gaps that so readily become politicised. Alfred Holt was also very interested in the *Conway* and was involved in its management. Blue Funnel (the popular name for Alfred Holt) was the destination for many of its cadets.

Conway boys tended to excel at Aberdovey. They were already involved in a physically demanding lifestyle—much more so than the apprentices from industry who made up some of the numbers. Part of the course was to spend a few days on a small sailing ship called the *Garibaldi*. She had begun life as an Italian onion boat and gave practical experience in boat handling. Again, *Conway* people had an advantage, for boat handling was part of their daily life. It was on the *Garibaldi* that I discovered my tendency to seasickness, a condition that was to remain for the rest of my time at sea.

Walking was also a key part of the programme. Beginning with five-mile walks, these were gradually extended through the month until towards the end we did a twenty-eight mile marathon. This is the longest I have ever done, or have any ambition to do! My chief recollection is of being rather tired and footsore at the end. Other activities included learning to map read, and use of a compass in the open country, also operating in the open at night. All in all, a varied and healthy programme, it is hardly surprising they have multiplied, some as mountain schools.

Three weeks before the end of term a 'still' was sounded. A 'still' was a brief bugle call that preceded a shouted verbal message or instruction, given usually by the officer of the watch. Provided there was silence, these messages could be heard throughout the ship. At the end of the announcement the bugle sounded 'carry on'. On this occasion it was to call for three cheers for going home three weeks to the day. The response was feeble in the extreme. The same exercise was repeated at two weeks and one week, then daily to the final three cheers for going home today. The response improved steadily as the time shortened, with the final one resulting in a deafening roar. Quite how the tradition started no one seemed to know, but it was much liked.

Succeeding terms saw one climb the ladder of seniority step-by-step, accruing along the way a succession of tiny privileges, which were nonetheless carefully guarded and implemented. One such was gaining the right to move freely through the ship without having to ask for 'top' at an invisible line. One's own section of living space was carefully defined, as were all the others. To move into someone else's living space required junior cadets to ask for permission. It was called 'asking for top', and was rather tedious, especially for new chums who didn't even know where the lines of demarcation were.

Returning to the ship as a fifth term, almost the first move was to scan the lists to see whether a 'rate' had been given—that is, whether promotion to junior cadet captain had been awarded. If it had, a gold stripe had to be secured, which then needed to be sewn onto the left hand sleeve. Boys who didn't know one end of a needle from another could be seen busily stitching the prized emblem on. Rates to one or other of the boats were very popular, though most were to the various tops, where the junior c.c. assisted his senior in the managing of the couple of dozen cadets who formed the top.

After the first term, which in many ways was an extended induction, cadets graduated to a new top each term, except for the little fellows, who were sent to one of the two mizzen tops. Being one such, I found myself in port mizzen and stayed there for the next three terms. Returning to begin my fifth term I was naturally delighted to find I had become the junior c.c. of starboard mizzen. I think it is probably true that if I was pleased, my parents were more so. Come the last term, I migrated back to port mitten as its senior c.c. My predecessor in that role had been one David Brown, who gained some fame as the longest serving cadet in the history of the ship. His father was a captain in the R.N. and David was determined to follow an R.N. career, but had difficulty with the exams. So he just kept taking them till he passed! Neither this, nor his diminutive size, prevented him from progressing once in the navy. David finished up as Vice Admiral Sir David Brown K.C.B.E.

The sixth and last term, the search was the same—junior c.c.'s gained senior status, or unrated fifth term cadets gained a rate in their last. Those becoming senior c.c.'s removed the smaller gold band and replaced it with a larger, slightly more elaborate one. More privileges attached to the office, such as access to what was called a P.O.'s mess. This was a small room on the lower deck with some seating and a few shelves, though bang through the middle of it passed the mainmast which reduced the effective space substantially. Another mark of rank was the right to use a companionway from the lower to the orlop deck. This was closed even to junior c.c.'s. These minute marks of status were used with pride, to which I succumbed no less than others. It should have been an object lesson in how human beings can be moved by such trivial tokens.

Because so much of the routine and daily operation of the ship was devolved to cadet captains, they were given quite formidable powers and could expect the support of the executive officers, who in fair measure depended on their performance. It was, of course, excellent training for the boys themselves, and for the most part they conducted themselves responsibly.

Once the ship had been left, and life at sea proper began, all were once again on the same footing, starting at the bottom of the ladder. Having been a cadet captain counted for nothing in this real world. But then progress through life is marked by frequent returns to the bottom of various ladders, before hopefully leaving them behind for good!

By current standards, there was a great deal that would be unacceptable today to the guardians of our education system. Not to mention the many openings, such as lack of safety, that would be seen to exist by the litigiously minded, avid for an opportunity to sue. Probably at least half today's European regulations governing safety, and much else, were being breached on a daily basis. There was austerity, made more stringent by wartime conditions, but there was both a fullness and a purposefulness in our lives. We knew what we were aiming for, and believed it to be a worthwhile goal. At some level of consciousness also, we recognised that all that was being done was with our longer-term interests at heart.

That the ever increasing move to enforce greater safety, combined with a marked tendency on the part of many to rush to litigation at the drop of a hat, is in the interest of young people, must be very much doubted. Already schools are shying away from anything that might have the slightest risk for their pupils. Teachers, understandably, ask why they should expose themselves to being sued should the slightest incident occur. Denied anything that could properly be called adventure, the child is the loser.

Also, the present attempts to provide a sanction-free environment for the rearing of children is a disaster. Love seeks a child's best, not its immediate gratification. One of the greatest gifts parents can give their children is a disciplined framework, within the security of which they can develop their values and outlook. Instead, there is a presumption that they must be allowed 'to do their own thing'. Not surprisingly, as they move to adolescence and adulthood, they assume that they can continue to do so, irrespective of others' rights and interests. This brings them into conflict with the law. The result is a prison population today of 75,000 and rising. In the 1950's it was some 18,000. New prisons are being built to meet government's projected increase of numbers beyond 100,000—this despite the alternatives now widely used: community service, tagging, suspended sentences, early release and much else. Every year tens of thousands of young people find their lives disadvantaged by a criminal record. At some point the pendulum will begin to swing back. For the sake of our children it must be hoped it will be soon.

By the standards of just a century earlier our lives, by comparison, were ones of undreamt of luxury. As noted above, when as a ship of the line the *Conway* was commissioned for a three-month voyage, she would have a crew of 850, not 250 cadets. Whereas she was victualled and watered, in those days, to last for months, we were bringing off stores and water daily; also, she was originally equipped with a space consuming complement of 92 guns and all the supporting equipment of cannon, powder, ropes, etc.—we were free of all that. Life on board in the 1840's was a very different matter from life on board in the 1940's and we had some awareness of this. It was perhaps one of the gains of actually living and working on the ship, that those conditions could be pictured more readily.

Over the years I have met with scores of 'old *Conways*', some older, some younger, many who were on the ship at the same time as myself. I have yet to meet one who did not hold the ship in warm affection, an affection that I share fully. Many of my year renewed acquaintances and friendships at a 1994 reunion to mark the fifty years since we joined the ship, and another one in 1996 to record a half-century since leaving it. For many, if not most, it was the first time our paths had crossed in the whole of that time. That we had altered out of all recognition goes without saying. One thing, though, hadn't changed, and that was voices. The tone a little deeper, perhaps, but all the vocal characteristics that had identified the boy then still characterised the man now. There was also a universal recognition that in preparing us for the real world, the ship served us well.

OFF TO SEA

In July 1946, along with most of my term, I bade farewell for the last time to my training ship, and did so with mixed emotions. If life on board her had been hard, at least by contemporary standards, it had also been happy and fulfilling. Now sixteen and anxious to get to grips with the larger world that awaited, the price for doing so was to leave behind the exalted status of a senior cadet captain, and be transformed overnight into a first year sea going cadet. No humbler state is known to marine life. At least it was the first step on a career ladder which, if all went well, would lead to command of some great ocean liner, all decked out in a uniform (strictly livery) liberally decorated with gold.

School holidays now a thing of the past, I had written to advise the Union Castle Mail Steamship Co. Ltd., of my availability. They having earlier agreed to offer me a cadetship, it didn't take long for them to send instructions for me to join the *Sandown Castle*. One of their oldest general cargo carriers, built in 1921, she was already twenty-five years old and one of the very few still fuelled by coal. This was not the most exciting ship in which to begin a seafaring life, but cadets didn't dictate their preferences! In the event I went down with jaundice before being due to leave home, and it was the *Sandown*'s misfortune to have to sail without me!

Now recovered, there arrived in the post fresh instructions, this time to join the *Gerusalemme* in Madras harbour. Included was a ticket to take a train to Southampton, and another to board one of Royal Mail's latest passenger ships, the *R.M.S. Andes* to Bombay, from there to organise a train to Madras. Whilst myself confident, in the way teenagers can be, that I could handle whatever arrangements were necessary, my parents were glad to find that there were a few other officers heading for the same destination, also to relieve their peers, and who had completed an eighteen month tour of duty. I, along with all the others, went out on the basis that it could be two years before returning home. In the event it proved to be only seven months.

The *Gerusalemme* was not a Union Castle ship, but belonged to an Italian company called Lloyd Triestino. When in 1943 the Italians quit the war, the British decided they could use some extra shipping and simply confiscated it.

Built shortly after the end of the First World War, she was oil fired and used extensively as a pilgrim ship running the faithful to Jeddah, from where they went on to Mecca. Only about 7,500 tons, she was a small passenger boat, and with quite beautiful public rooms for first class, finished in a baroque style that the Italians brought off magnificently. Life below first class was organised for economy rather than splendour. Having been in the warm Far Eastern waters for over two years without benefit of a dry docking, below the water line was a solid mass of marine weeds which stretched up to eighteen inches from the sides and bottom. Never the fastest ship afloat, this growth slowed her down to the point where, on a good day with a following wind, she could make all of six knots! Put under U.C. management, she had earlier been converted to a fine hospital ship with several well-equipped wards, operating theatre, and state of the art equipment for the mid-1940's.

Arriving in Southampton, I duly boarded the *Andes*, found my accommodation and settled in for a fortnight's passage. It was early post war and she hadn't been reconverted back to a passenger ship after serving as a troop carrier, so she was not overly luxurious, but positively sumptuous by *Conway* standards. No problem for me, but a source of acute distress to many, she was a 'dry' ship. No alcohol was available. It was on her that I was introduced to tomato juice, a drink that was to remain a lifelong favourite. Many of the passengers were old India hands returning to their posts after some leave. It was shortly before Independence was to be declared the following year, and there was much uncertainty about longer-term futures. From them I picked up some useful information. You won't see many Indians with grey hair, I was told. Average life expectancy was under thirty. Give money to one beggar, of whom there were vast numbers, and you will be surrounded by fifty in seconds, others promised. "Before we are within five miles of Bombay you will be able to smell it," assured another. They all proved more or less right.

Whether a couple of weeks spent in leisurely comfort soaking up the sun was the best way for a youngster to begin his working life, must be thought an open question. It was, however, very agreeable while it lasted. Finally we docked in Bombay. For many passengers it was the end of the line, for us a brief pause in our onward journey. The immediate need was to book a train for the day and a half journey to Madras. This process was designed less to speed the passenger and more to reduce unemployment. It began with a queue to get a piece of paper authorising, and taking payment for, a ticket. But the paper was not the ticket itself. Armed with this vital document, one was able to join another queue to another desk where the voucher was examined with meticulous care. The clerk might never have seen such a thing before. Finally, satisfied it was genuine, and with the air of a man putting his career on the line, the much sought after ticket was passed over, the voucher surrendered. It was better not to be in a hurry when planning to travel on the Indian railway, for the queues moved only at a gentle pace.

Secreting this passport to travel most carefully, the thought of going through the whole procedure again was not to be borne. It was then a simple case of waiting a day or so for the designated rolling stock to surface. Being white, it was unthinkable to travel other than first class, even for cadets. Reaching the train and locating the exact seat, all as stated on the ticket, was my introduction to what constituted first. Despite being an overnight journey, there was no provision for sleeping in a very run of the mill compartment with seriously tired upholstery. But there was a loo and washbasin adjoining, which had almost certainly been cleaned at some point during the previous several months. It was only when it was noted that third class was an open truck with standing room only, that it was realised that to be awarded first class was indeed a privilege of some magnitude. Kipling had it about right when he said, "East of Suez, where the best is like the worst."

Safely installed, the train got underway and headed for Madras, crossing much undifferentiated countryside and many villages each like the other. A number of stops were made at larger centres. At each, the carriages were bombarded by traders selling their wares. Those offering food and drink did good business, for there were no catering facilities on the train itself. Disembarking at Madras station, a taxi quickly took us to the quayside and offered a first view of the elderly and rather dignified lady I had come to serve, anchored in the harbour. Painted white all over with a green band around the entire hull, identified her as a hospital ship. Before long a motor lifeboat arrived to take us on board. Coxing this boat was to become one of my regular jobs, aided by a crew of three Lascars.

Reporting to the Chief Officer, I learnt I was the only cadet, an unusual arrangement. Most ships carried up to half a dozen for the very practical reason that they were cheap labour. It meant I had my own cabin and shared a Goanese steward with two other officers. As I subsequently discovered, this was not the way things were usually organised. Notionally officers, cadets were usually treated as the lowest form of sea life, given the worst jobs and worked the longest hours. They did not have individual cabins, still less the services of a personal steward. I had landed in the lap of luxury.

The ship carried a substantial headcount. The ship's officers were English, the crew Lascar up to and including the Head Serang (Bosun), the catering and stewards, Goanese. The hospital side was headed by an army doctor with the rank of colonel; under him were a number of junior doctors, mainly Anglo Indian and supported by a large contingent of nurses, also all Anglo Indian and headed by a matron. In colour, some of the nurses were indistinguishable from white, through to dark brown. Mainly young, and some very attractive, they very quickly paired off with officers and doctors in relationships that mostly lasted till the ship was decommissioned.

All were under the command of the captain, one Aldous, a good seaman but who had an alcohol problem. During his time on the ship he was teetotal, but some year or two later I heard he had gone back to the bottle and been sacked. It rubbed with the colonel that he was subordinate to the captain, had much inferior accommodation, and had to sit at the captain's right hand in the dining saloon. They were oil and water—the colonel, polished, whose manners and bearing had been formed in the officer's mess over years; the captain, by contrast, was a rough diamond with language to match, who had learnt his seamanship in the hard school of sailing ships. But he knew the ship was his, and he commanded it, a state of affairs of which the colonel was left in no doubt.

Dinner was the chief focal point of the day. The dining saloon was a lovely room, the decor Italian baroque, brilliantly lit, spotlessly clean with beautifully laid tables. The food matched the surroundings, the Goans knew how to cook and the menu was varied. It was here that I learnt to appreciate curries. Prepared in the country and by the people who originated the dish, they were superb. I have never tasted their equal since. There was, among several Western choices, a curry dish every day, chiefly for the benefit of the Anglo Indian contingent. Everyone dressed to match the surroundings, officers in their No.10's, army officers in their best uniforms, the nurses likewise. Sometimes, chiefly weekends and when off duty, the nurses would wear saris and add delightful splashes of colour to the occasion. To all of this splendour there was one exception—the captain! He normally arrived after everyone else and took his place at the head of the chief table, dressed in a pair of canvas shorts he had made himself, a short sleeved open neck shirt, and a pair of rather tired slippers worn without the benefit of socks! It might have been interesting to listen to the conversation between the captain and the colonel. I suspect it may have been strained.

The ship, when not functioning as a hospital, lay quietly at anchor in Madras harbour, a few hundred yards from the quayside. Everywhere was kept spotlessly clean by a large crew with little else to do. In seven months the ship made only two real voyages, one running wounded prisoners of war to their home country, the other to return her to her owners. My own duties were not onerous, chiefly in charge of the boat which linked us with the shore, and which made several trips a day. I was given time to study, for in three years there was an exam to be faced, both written and oral. Study time was unique, in my experience, to the *Gerusalemme*; the general rule was that cadets were there to be exploited for their labour.

There were plenty of opportunities to go ashore, but only within the general area of the city. I, with most others, joined an exclusive club, only affordable because we were made honorary members. There, in comfortable colonial type surroundings, was a swimming pool, endless servants, daily papers, drinks and food. Life was not unduly stressed!

It was not unusual for temperatures to reach 100°F in the shade, this at a time when I was getting letters from home telling of a very hard winter and ongoing shortages of fuel. Having seen something of the lifestyle of the India hands, it was not surprising that at independence, when most were shipped back to England, they had a terrible time trying to adjust to the climate, the pace of life, the need to start doing things for themselves, and the loss of status. In India they had been little gods, whereas in England they were very ordinary citizens.

The poverty for multitudes was absolute. For many, their only home was a few square feet of pavement with perhaps a mat to separate them from the paving stones. Beggars in their thousands, some mutilated deliberately when still children to arouse a greater sympathy. Hunger was rampant, with precious little in the way of public services for those at the bottom of the heap. The problem was on so vast a scale, having existed since time immemorial, that the advantaged simply didn't see it. Their only concern was to ensure they didn't fall from their happier circumstances. For millions, life was nasty, brutish, and short.

Independence was declared in 1947 and there was a tangible air of expectancy. It could be picked up in the streets, sometimes with an aggressive quality. One day I was walking with a colleague, the third radio officer down a busy shopping street. (At 16 I was the youngest; he was 19, so we got on quite well together.) An Indian coming the other way spat at us as we passed. "What was that for?" I asked. "Because we are English," my companion replied. It was no doubt an accurate response.

Finally came the day when we were ordered to sea to collect some hundreds of Japanese P.O.W's, all wounded with varying degrees of severity, from Rangoon. Steam raised, we pulled out of the harbour, cleared the sea wall, and rang 'full ahead'. The old lady picked up her skirts and hurtled through the water at not less than six knots! An ageing tramp that left a few hours later and headed in the same direction overhauled us rapidly! En route we called at Singapore briefly; in late 1946 it hadn't evolved into the hugely prosperous metropolis of today.

From there we went on to Rangoon for a stay of some ten days whilst embarking the wounded men and some stores. The military were running the place and were very helpful, placing transport at our disposal. The most memorable recollection here was of a visit to the great Buddhist temple, the Shwe Dagon. The captain, who had made it possible for me to go, asked in return that I write a piece about it which he wanted to read. I still have it. Our next stop was Hong Kong, even then a vibrant city of contrasts. There was the financial and commercial centre with its modern high-rise buildings, but minutes' walk away from the traditional, crowded and cramped homes and markets of the majority. Back at sea we hit some rough weather proceeding up the east coast of China. A moment of interest was when the carpenter discovered that the collision bulkhead was badly rusted and effectively useless. Happily we didn't, in the event, collide with anything!

On board, the Japanese were docile, grateful to be going home, but apprehensive of their welcome once there. Japanese soldiers weren't supposed to be captured—they were expected to die fighting. To be taken prisoner was a shameful disgrace, even if wounded. The soldiers were accommodated in the wards of which there were several, but the walking wounded were allowed to exercise on deck. If one saw an officer approaching, he would bow deeply from the waist, swivel in his direction as he passed, remaining bowed, and continue in that state until he was out of sight. Such treatment was not good for the development of humility in a sixteen year old!

Even at six knots, we finally arrived at our destination—Kure. This is a port in the Southern part of Honshu and was a major submarine base during the war. As such it had received the frequent attentions of American bombers and was very severely damaged, the submarine pens being a vast heap of tangled steel. As we entered close waters, the pilot was picked up as usual and arrived unimpressively on the bridge. Unimpressively, because he was less a small man and more a minute one, with all the servility of the newly conquered, and a voice that singularly failed to inspire confidence. The captain looked hard at this party who was to take control of his ship, decided he wasn't, walked over to him, lifted him up and carried him bodily off the bridge. The pilot accepted without demur.

This meant Aldous would have to take his own ship through unknown and narrow waters and dock her without the benefit of tugs, for the tugmen spoke no English, and the captain most certainly spoke no Japanese. That he carried out the operation without a hitch spoke well for his seamanship, especially since he had never been to that part of the world previously. Had he damaged or put his ship aground, it wouldn't have read well in the report that he had thrown the duly appointed professional off the bridge! When a ship is coming into port, a log is kept of every move and every order, with the exact time of each, and is a job usually done by a cadet. I remember noting the time the pilot arrived on the bridge and the time he left. It didn't seem necessary to indicate the manner of his leaving—the smallness of the gap between his coming and going was sufficiently eloquent!

We spent about three weeks in port. (Things were not done with unnecessary haste in those days.) The prisoners were put ashore promptly enough, but since the *Gerusalemme* had no other pressing engagements, we lingered. It gave opportunity to see something of this far off country that had caused such continuous havoc in the East from the early 1930's onwards. The country is mountainous; a day's walk from the port was enough to take us into the hills, where it was like moving back in time. Farming methods, implements, homes, were all utterly basic. There could have been little change over centuries. Nothing was wasted; even human soil was collected and used as fertiliser. This was put into carts and taken to where it was to be used. Coming upon such a cart, it would invariably advertise its contents from some distance! Not something that bothered the farmer, but we tended to detour a little.

Kure is only about ten miles down the road from Hiroshima, so with the help of the American military who were running the country, we secured transport in the shape of a jeep to go there. The devastation was extensive, though the type of construction of much of the city lent itself to destruction by fire, lightweight and inflammable materials having been extensively used. Whole roads of residential housing effectively evaporated, with the road itself marked out only by tree stumps sticking up, blackened, about a foot out of the ground. That said, there was a reinforced concrete building very close to the epicentre of the blast which, though very badly damaged, was still standing.

Whilst the Americans were in control of everything through their military, the British did have some service contingents stationed in Kure. To my astonishment, up the gangway the day after we had arrived, came a chap in R.A.F. uniform, one Jeff Griffin. He lived about a hundred yards from my home! I wrote to my family on a very regular basis, and had advised that I would shortly be heading for Kure. My mother had mentioned this to Mrs Griffin, who wrote to her son who was based there. He in turn linked me up with Hill, the sometime head prefect of my old school. He too was in the R.A.F. Academically a very bright fellow, he had mastered the language and was acting as an interpreter. It was Hill who came with me to Hiroshima.

Perhaps this is the moment to touch on finance. My agreed rate of pay for my first year as cadet was £2-l0-0 a month (£2.50 in today's currency). The hours worked were those required; no overtime was payable to cadets, so there was nothing to discourage a lavish use of our time. Not a large sum even in those far off days, though it should he remembered that food and accommodation were provided. But this was very early post war, and all merchant seamen were paid danger money by the government, over and above the company stipend. In my case that was a further £7-10-0 a month—comparative riches. The justification for continuing this for a period after the war was that there were thousands of mines still scattered around the oceans of the world.

The real gain, however, came through our access to cigarettes, which, for several years, were the common currency of both Europe and the East. On the ship they were packaged in airtight tins of fifty by leading manufacturers and cost 10d (4p). That meant one pound would buy 1,200 cigarettes! Ashore, their worth multiplied by a very large factor, making even the humblest cadet remarkably wealthy! There was a limit to the number that could be bought on board—200 a week. As one of the very few that didn't smoke, my whole ration was converted to a means of exchange. That this practice, though perfectly legal, wasn't helpful to the economies of struggling nations must be assumed. Lamentably, it was not a consideration that loomed large—if it loomed at all. The upshot was that I arrived home laden with things Japanese for my family, everything from chopsticks to elaborately decorated kimonos, with porcelain tea sets and wooden artefacts in between.

When our stay ended, we set off for Madras calling again at Hong Kong and Singapore. It had been decided by the chief officer that I would stand watch with him. As the most senior of the watch keepers (the captain didn't have a watch) he had the best one, the 4-8. There was only one minus, a call at 3-45 a.m., but coming off at 8-00 a.m. was handy for having a proper breakfast at a proper time. One was then off duty (at least in theory) until 4-00 p.m. Being relieved at 8-00 p.m. enabled us to have dinner in the saloon and the possibility of about six hours of unbroken sleep. His decision to have me with him was less than disinterested—it meant he could take his ease in the chartroom once in open waters, using me on the bridge as his eyes! The chief downside of watch keeping at sea is that it is, inevitably, seven days a week, not excluding Christmas day.

We were anchored in Madras when, one day, I received an invitation from the Chief Engineer to join him in his cabin for a drink after dinner. It was very unusual for someone as junior as a cadet to be invited to socialise with an officer of such senior rank, but once given was not to be refused. Appearing at the agreed time, he had minerals and sweets at the ready, for he knew I didn't drink. (My enthusiasm for wine was to develop some time later!) Conversation flowed quite affably on generalities when at some point he asked if I had a girlfriend. Looking back, I imagine he may have taken heart when the answer was "no". From there on the questions became increasingly personal and it registered why the invite had been extended! When I indicated that it was time for me to leave, he accepted without question, though it must be supposed with an element of disappointment. As a person I always found him pleasant, slightly world weary, and probably not too far off retirement. Nothing further was ever said by him or me, and the normal relationship that could he expected to subsist between a cadet and a senior officer obtained.

Apart from one other short trip of no great moment, that was it. We settled back into the harbour routine awaiting orders that never came, until about February1947, when instructions were received to strip the ship of its hospital equipment and then proceed to Venice. The ship was to be handed back to its rightful owners. All the Anglo Indians were disembarked, the girls with much tearfulness, hopes of marriage unfulfilled, the rather less rewarding promise of maintained contact freely given and quickly broken.

The Anglo Indians had a hard time of it. They were not readily accepted properly by either Indians or English, but dwelt in a sort of no-man's land. It somehow seemed only to add to the inequity, because some of the girls were quite lovely in both appearance and nature. The removal of the equipment was a melancholy affair. Large open barges, used for the movement of all manner of goods including coal, drew up alongside the ship. Into this filth were thrown mattresses, bedding, various equipment including large, modern Kelvinator fridges that had graced each ward, beds, tables, storage cupboards and all the impedimenta of a hospital. I begged the chief officer to let me have one of the fridges and I would be responsible for packing and getting it back to England. He refused, saying, "They aren't mine to give or to sell." This unhappy episode ended, we set sail for Venice and the head office of the rightful owners, Lloyd Triestino.

Arriving after a slow, even stately voyage, we found ourselves steaming up the Grand Canal to our berth. Company officials boarded, and in a little handing over ceremony, the victims thanked us for returning what we had earlier stolen. Apart from the festoons of flora below the water line, I rather suspect she was in better condition than when she was taken. Again, there was no urgency—government was paying, so we spent a very agreeable week in this unique city, taking in all the sights—St. Marks Cathedral, the Campanile, the Doge's palace; we saw exquisite glass being blown into beautiful shapes, mosaic designs being formed, and much else. The endless bridges over equally endless canals became rather tedious, and it was clear that the small canals away from the central areas were really just open sewers. That allowed, it was a place full of history and priceless treasures. As for the ship, she was overhauled and re-converted back to her former status, and was worked for several more years.

Time came to go, so we boarded the train for Paris via Switzerland and the Simplon Tunnel. Some of the Swiss scenery was just breathtaking. Our stay in Paris was about three days, being lodged in a small hotel. Virtually the whole of the time we were free to do as we wished. Food was a big problem throughout large areas of Europe, including Paris, so it was probably not surprising that horsemeat was on the menu. It would have been unreasonable not to take the chance to visit the Folies Bergere. With some anticipation I paid my entrance fee and was shown to my seat by an appropriately underdressed female—which seemed quite a good start to the proceedings until, disconcertingly, she stood her ground shaking an outstretched, open hand, until even I got the message and found some coins to ease its shaking and induce a withdrawal. In my confusion at being attacked in this way, I probably gave her far too much, for her fixed and hostile glare gave way to an easy smile and, if memory serves, even a "merci". But, no shrinking violet, she. The programme was titillatingly erotic, though in the porn-laden world of today it would seem hopelessly tame. It didn't appear so to one sixteen-year-old youth at the time.

Once more a train was boarded for the relatively short journey to the coast, where we transferred to a ferry and then entrained for London where we signed off. So ended the first voyage in my chosen career. It was very different from the normal experience of first year cadets, a more kindly introduction than was good for me, but that presented an opportunity to see something of the Far East, which the company I had joined, in normal times, never served. From here on life was to be very different, but not before a short leave to be spent with my family, and where I could dispose of all my ill-gotten gains. At a time when foreign travel was unthinkable, and arrangements for it nonexistent, I had been fortunate enough to see a useful slice of some far-flung countries, and found myself an object of some curiosity and even envy, all mostly at government expense. I was shortly to find a very sharp difference in the approach when a profit and loss company was to pick up the bill.

OF OTHER SHIPS AND HURRICANES

Early in May instructions arrived to report to the *Drakensberg Castle* on the 15th. The only memorable bit of the journey was the taxi to the Victoria Dock in London where the ship was berthed. This was a part of the dock system known as the 'Royals', and was some distance from Euston station. It was outside the controlled fare area of London, so taxis could charge whatever they liked—in the event, £2. With my large metal trunk and other impedimenta, no other mode of transport was feasible. The shock, however, of that moment registers still. Almost a week's pay for just one taxi ride was hugely disproportionate to my earnings.

Arriving on board and reporting to the chief officer, his baleful response was, "Get your boiler suit on and report to the bosun!" This was not the way things had been in the recent past, but given the assorted expletives attached to the order, it seemed likely to be counter productive to ask to be directed to my accommodation. It didn't prove too difficult to find. There were four of us, all in the same cabin. The others had arrived earlier and were already working. Changed, I sought out the bosun who directed me to the bilges where my peers were toiling. All manner of nauseous material, including dead rats, found their way to this unappealing area and had to be cleared periodically. Bosuns generally found it convenient to use cadets for such labours. Ordinary seamen could kick, whereas cadets with long-term careers in front of them were unlikely to wish to prejudice their futures with bolshy behaviour. This was not an auspicious start.

The *Drakensberg* was a super empire boat, 10,000 tons and of all welded construction, built during the war as Britain's answer to the American Liberty ships. She carried more cargo than was average for the time, and boasted a 50-ton heavy lift derrick. Reflecting the urgency of the period, she was a bit rough at the edges, but of far better construction, and significantly stronger than her Liberty counterparts. In fairness to the Americans, they were, at their peak, completing three ships a day. Nothing remotely approaching that was ever achieved by British yards. We were to be glad of her robust build in due time.

My peers proved to be a straightforward bunch, though names now escape me, and we rubbed along well enough. One thing the sea teaches is not to make waves with your colleagues—you may be in a relatively confined space with one another for months together. Since it was not possible to get very far from your worst enemy, it was better not to have enemies. Round pegs in round holes made for a more comfortable life. One thing as cadets we had to get used to, was wearing boiler suits or other workwear during the day and changing into a smart uniform for meals, for we dined with all the officers and passengers. This had the occasional side effect of our being ignored by passengers when working, and being pleasantly acknowledged when smartly turned out. To such more class-conscious folk, there was sometimes embarrassment when it finally registered that we were one and the same person!

The captain was a Welshman called Lloyd. Large of ego and small of stature, he was universally known throughout the Union Castle fleet as 'Batchy Lloyd'. Though not mentally adrift, he was a man of many minor eccentricities—one of which was his rather baroque manner of writing, an example of which is still in my discharge book. It could not be said we gelled very well; he didn't like me and took no special pains to hide it. Arriving at Suez, it emerged he was working a fiddle with the bumboat men. He allowed only a small number of non-competing ones on board against their making a useful payment to him personally. This meant they were able to up their prices, and the crew and passengers effectively therefore paid the bribe through enhanced charges.

This did nothing to improve our relationship. He took his revenge when at the end of the voyage he stamped my discharge book with a 'good' for ability. Now, I have never thought I was ever better than 'good' at most things in this world, and not always that, so was perfectly happy, especially as I got a 'very good' for conduct. Somehow or other—it certainly wasn't me—word reached the ears of the Navigating and Engineering Officers' Union of which I was a member. Their representative, a Mr Benson—I remember him well—was incandescent. He explained to me that in the arcane world of discharge books, a 'good' was a disaster, a major blot on my record that would follow me down the years. Quoth he: "It has got to be changed!"

I rather suspect this may not have been the first time he had crossed swords with the singular captain Lloyd. Anyway, he took up the cudgels on my behalf and persuaded the powers that be to change it. So, there in my discharge book, is the cancelled entry with its replacement immediately below. Still today, when told, which isn't very often, that something I have done is 'good', I am not sure whether that is a compliment or a reprimand! I was to endure the surprising Mr

Lloyd for two more voyages, though he never again tried to pass me off with a 'good'. In the way of the sea we coped, though as captain the balance of advantage lay firmly with him.

Our first voyage, once loaded with a mixed cargo that included cars and other desirable consumer durables, was to South Africa. The war had virtually bankrupted us as a nation so it was a time of export or die. Our cars in 1947 were still essentially pre-war models with a few minor cosmetic changes, but there was obviously a market for them. The run was without incident. I was put on the 12-4 watch with the second officer. It was the least liked because it was never possible to get more than about four hours of unbroken sleep. Some compensation was found in the second officer, a very likeable chap, and we got on very well together. Once in the open sea, watch-keeping is not the most exciting activity; water around the world tends to look much the same, so there were many hours spent chatting. He also gave me some unofficial help towards mastering the esoteric arts of navigation and seamanship. His enthusiasm for his captain was as great as my own, and he developed his own approach to remedying some of the slights he had to endure from that quarter.

The captain's accommodation was immediately under the bridge, and he was known to be a light sleeper. On one occasion, around two in the morning, the second took off one shoe and stamped heavily with his one shod foot over where the bed lay below, and silently with the other, rightly calculating that once awake, Lloyd would he puzzled by the irregular sound instead of the expected alternate footsteps. The captain arrived on the bridge inflamed with both ire and curiosity. With a remarkably straight face the second explained, in the most moderate terms, that he had hurt his foot and had had to take off his shoe. That the yarn was believed must be thought remote, but no obvious means of exacting retribution lay immediately to hand.

On another occasion, again at some ungodly hour, the second found some heavy artefact that he tipped down the companionway, and which was adjacent to the captain's suite. It made a frightful racket and brought the captain lurching from his slumbers, wondering perhaps if his ship was blowing up. The second was profusely apologetic, explaining that he was carrying it down when it slipped from his grasp. By such means do those who hold themselves maligned by their superiors level the playing field. Managers need to know that genuine support must be won. It can never he compelled.

Sometime earlier I had joined a small Christian organisation called 'Living Links'. It had representatives in many ports worldwide, and when a member arrived, someone from the organisation would make contact and offer friendship.

The 'link' in Capetown was one George Young, at that time the shipping editor of the *Cape Times*. Recently demobbed from the South African air force in which he had served during the war, he had returned to his journalistic profession. Though never a sailor, he had a passion for things of the sea and was a walking encyclopaedia of the marine world. In his early thirties, he had married a couple of years previously, and the first babe had surfaced only weeks earlier.

We hit it off in the way of these things, and George invited me to his home where I met his delightful wife, Pixie. He was very proud of the new arrival; he picked up the baby and handed him to me to hold. I can still recall the waves of anxiety from Pixie as she saw this callow, unknown teenager holding all that was most precious in her world. After a brief moment I handed baby Robert back to his mum—to her infinite relief. Robert today is a top executive of South Africa's main shipping company. Thus began a friendship that persisted until George's recent death, having achieved a very respectable eighty-eight years. A couple of years after this first meeting, George was to offer me a job as a trainee journalist on the *Cape Times*, an offer I was to come very close to accepting. From this point on I linked up with the Youngs each time we docked in the lovely city of Capetown.

Leaving Capetown, we progressed along the coast calling at Port Elizabeth, East London, and the major port of Durban. In Durban I was met by an uncle I had never seen before, my mother's elder brother. He had served in the First World War and decided to emigrate to South Africa where he aimed to make his fortune. All his hopes had turned to dust. A carpenter by trade, he had gone into partnership with a man he had met en route south, but who disappeared with his investment on arrival. Following this unhappy episode he stuck to his trade. By the time we met he was in his later fifties, his family having grown up and with a wife who had ballooned into a woman of enormous girth—a woman for whom movement of any sort was a burden and a challenge. They were lodged in depressing circumstances. On returning home and reporting my findings, my mother was shocked; she had it fixed in her mind that he was a roaring success. Correspondence between them was sparse—perhaps a letter every several years.

Heading North up the East coast, we called at what was then Lourenço Marques under Portuguese control, Mombassa, Dar-es-Salaam, Zanzibar, Port Sudan, and through the Suez Canal, disbursing and collecting cargo as we went. Our wayward captain managed to upset one of the cooks rather badly. The cook responded by going for him with a meat cleaver. Overpowered before doing any mortal damage, he was locked away until our next port of call. The ship had radioed ahead to Dar-es-Salaam to ask that police be available to take the man in charge. The place had no facilities for docking, so we anchored. Police came aboard and took the fellow away, but it created a problem for the authorities. It was a British colony with the usual small contingent of white administrators. There was a prison for blacks, but our man was white and there were no arrangements for white felons; it wasn't expected that there would be any! It was unthinkable to put him in the black prison. In the event we upped anchor after a brief stay and I don't know what became of him.

At Lourenço Marques I had a sports jacket stolen from my cabin. It had been on my bunk which was immediately under a porthole, and which hadn't been properly closed. Reporting it to a Portuguese man in charge of the dockers who were working the ship, he at once grabbed one of them and started belabouring him with a rope's end, demanding to know who had taken it. The man didn't respond. I never did get my jacket back, but did regret reporting it. There is something very distasteful and humiliating about one man beating another in general view. Noticeably, the black docker accepted his treatment with absolute passivity. Clearly, if not routine, it was a common occurrence.

Passing through the Suez Canal and arriving at Port Said, the captain's entrepreneurial arrangements came into play. His orders were that, his chosen traders aboard, all others were to be repelled. To this end hoses were rigged up around the ship (we were tied to buoys, not docked) and those who rejected verbal advice to disperse were hosed. Water did nothing to enhance their goods and the imprecations from the discomfited traders were fearful as they stood off from the ship.

Corruption was and remains rife, and runs through all levels of Egyptian society. The pilots at this time were European, but had Egyptian assistants. These last were among the more highly paid professionals. They sought nothing for themselves, of course, but invariably had relatives in difficult circumstances that would appreciate a little help! Tugboat men had to be paid off or they would put a dent in the ship's side. Those who tied us up would cut our ropes if they weren't 'fixed'. Later, the authorities decided a policeman had to be placed on every ship during her stay, and even he had to be bought or else would use his powers officiously. It was all so short sighted, because such was the reputation of the place that stores, etc., were only bought there if desperate. The risk of being short changed was too great.

Into the Mediterranean, our next stop was Barcelona. Franco was at the height of his power in a country that was still blighted from the after-effects of the civil war. Church and state worked very closely together, and there was abject poverty for the majority. Criticism was carefully muted and then only when there was no possibility of being overheard. A small number of us decided we ought to go to a bullfight; it was, after all, the national sport and hugely popular. It soon became clear that the odds were heavily loaded against the bull, and the whole spectacle one of the utmost cruelty. At one point one of the matadors got into difficulty, at which our English contingent cheered. This produced hostile looks from all around us, which argued for greater discretion. Shortly after, two of us left. It was a horrible business with nothing to justify calling it a sport. As we left, we passed through the area where the dead bulls were taken, and where they were in process of being cut up. Not a pretty sight.

Returning to England, we docked at Newport after an almost exactly four-month voyage. There was no opportunity to go home, for I was signed on for the next trip straight away. The practice was, that on joining a ship, articles were signed which allowed the company to take up to two years before returning to the U.K. If, however, the ship docked anywhere on the U.K. coastline before the two years, the articles were broken and fresh ones had to be signed. This time we were headed for Newfoundland, New York, Baltimore, and Philadelphia, before sailing for South Africa, again returning up the west coast of Africa. In Newfoundland we docked in Cornerbrook, a frontier style town whose only justification for existing was logging and the making of paper. It was a bleak place, and once the huge bales of newsprint were aboard we moved on.

New York was a very different matter. Its famous skyline promised excitement, but close up it was better to see it by night. After years of a blacked out wartime England, the vast and colourful array of neon and flashing lights was captivating. One hoarding particularly fascinated me. It was an advert for Camel cigarettes. The girl was holding a cigarette, her mouth shaped into an 'O' and blew smoke rings every few seconds. All was movement, bustle and vibrancy, the latest tunes played from a score of outlets and the dollar reigned supreme. By day it was all rather different—there was litter around in even the most prestigious parts such as Times Square, and once off the centre, places like Maddison Square Gardens, it could become quite squalid. The underground, too, was noisy and dirty. Ethnically it was as multiracial as London is today. It's a city dedicated to the worship of mammon, but paradoxically has the largest cathedral in the world—St. John the Divine, being built (and still is!) in the Harlem district.

From New York we headed for Philadelphia followed by Baltimore. Both cities could only be reached navigating some narrow waters, and we had pilots on board for much of the time. They were typical, large industrial centres, the buildings covered in the soot and grime that were the norm for urban centres in the forties. We were there to collect a load of their latest cars for the South African market. Now, for a seventeen-year-old lad, this was a cargo that dreams were made of. Large, multi-coloured, streamlined and heavily chromed, they were a tremendous contrast to the largely black, utilitarian 10 h.p. saloons that were the staple of the British market. Cadets were invariably deployed on cargo loading duties, so there was every opportunity to examine them at close quarters—Packards, Studebakers, Hudsons, Oldsmobiles, Chevrolets, Buicks—they and others were all there. For a period I knew every American car by year, make and model. Each year there would be some modifications to every car, even if it were only to change some of the chrome bits and thus enable the manufacturer to talk about the 'new model'. At Baltimore I linked up with an uncle, my mother's younger brother. An engineer with what later became British Airways, he had been seconded to the States. His stay there was brief; by the time we docked in Baltimore again he had returned to the U.K.

Fully laden with our handsome cargo, we set sail for Capetown. Before long the weather deteriorated and a storm set in. With conditions looking to worsen, everything was tightly battened down. A little later a hurricane developed, which, as is invariably the case, we were able to skirt because of sufficient warning. The ship slowed to the point where she was just able to keep head to wind; any faster and she would have pounded herself to bits. Visibility fell to about nil, largely due to the continuous foam caught and raised by enormously powerful winds. Speech on the bridge was limited to cupping hands to ear and yelling, such was the sound level generated by the wind in the rigging.

It was a majestic scene of transcendent and primeval force that held me spellbound. I had never seen anything remotely approaching it, nor have since. The ship was thrown about like a cork as it rode the waves. It was only later that I realised just how tiring it could be hour after hour, continually adjusting to meet the substantially changing deck beneath one's feet. Seasickness had been my companion ever since those few days in Cardigan Bay on the *Garibaldi*. But such was this experience that it didn't trouble me at all.

In time we moved into quieter waters, and the rest of the voyage was uneventful. Docking in Capetown and opening the hatches, a scene of devastation was revealed. In three of the holds forward of the bridge, all the 'tween decks had collapsed, each onto the next below. Steel girders which had supported hatch covers had pierced cars like so many arrows. Others had been crushed by collapsing deckheads. Not a single car survived from those holds. Journalists, photographers, official and unofficial, insurance inspectors and loss adjusters and company officials, all descended on the ship. The chief officer was responsible for cargo stowage and was cross-examined several times, but exonerated from any blame. It was finally put down to 'an act of God' and the insurers paid up.

What was striking was that no one on the ship had heard a single sound as the steel decks collapsed, though they must have made a hefty noise, such was the fury of the winds. It was well that the double bottom held, for had the ship foundered there would have been no survivors in those conditions. When dry-docked later the steel ribs onto which the plates were welded all showed up very plainly, for the plates were all severely indented either side of the ribs. Nevertheless the ship lived on for a number of years doing good work before finally being broken up.

The rest of that voyage was uneventful. My third and last trip on the *Drakensberg* was similar—America, Africa, though returning via the East Coast. The slippery Mr Lloyd moved to another ship with few regrets. His replacement, Captain Dexter McKenzie, was a dour Scot who seemed to find more consolation in the minuses of life than the plusses. Not a man given to taking excessive risk, he quickly got labelled 'Daring Dexter'. It was enough for D.D. to see the coastline in the far distance to come from full speed to 'half ahead'. He assured his officers that he was certain the company would prefer a ship safely docked slowly, than speedily run aground. No doubt they would, but the consensus was that the company would probably prefer the ship to be safely docked speedily! And even if they didn't, we would! At least he was straightforward and his people knew where they stood with him.

At the end of that voyage I had a couple of weeks leave and returned home laden with foodstuffs. Strict rationing was in force, and all such were welcomed gladly. The other requirement was for nylon stockings. Up to twelve pairs could be brought in without a licence, and I had been given careful instructions on sizes, style and colour. Mother, sister, aunts, aunty Thomasina Cobbley—all were in line! Purchasing the things was something else, and gave the shop girls some fun. I think, on balance, they probably accepted that I was possibly too young to be a transvestite, and really was buying on behalf of others!

My service on the *Drakensberg* ended, the next ship was different again. The *Richmond Castle*, built just before the war in 1938, equipped with diesel engines and refrigerated holds, was a little less than 8,000 tons. Good looking, as were all purpose built ships of the Union Castle, she was designed for the soft fruit trade with South Africa. General cargo out, and fruit home was the intended use—which is more or less the way it worked out. With only two cadets this time, we shared a cabin, and in the way of these things, despite my gaining seniority as time passed, my opposite number had more sea time, so I remained the junior. I was to complete seven voyages, each much like the other, almost like a bus service! Sometimes down to the Cape and straight back, the west coast both ways. Sometimes, sailing round the coast to Durban and carrying on up the east coast, calling at the same collection of ports as previously mentioned, through Suez and the Med. to home. Certainly this latter schedule was more interesting.

The captain was J. Sowden, an agreeable chap, whose chief objective seemed to be a hassle free life. He wasn't much given to taking initiatives in case they went wrong. If you don't stick your head above the parapet, it won't get knocked off! He was always, and said as much, aware that Head Office had a long reach. His hobby was carpentry. As soon as we had cleared the Bay of Biscay, out would come his carpenter's bench and tools, all set up on his private deck. He would then spend most of the day making various items, and to a pretty professional standard. I rather suspect that his entire house was very probably furnished with his own products. This would continue until we came within range of the Cape rollers. I heard some years later that he had died quite suddenly of a heart attack.

By this time I had picked up a modest typing skill, albeit with two fingers, and found myself doing quite a lot of secretarial work. It isn't entirely clear how this would forward my knowledge of the sea, but I quite enjoyed it nonetheless. Once a year cadets took a written exam set by some board or other, and the company was required to make time available to sit it. That is all they did make time for! Mine were all done during voyages, but it was very much up to the individual boy to set his own study plan, buy his own books, and generally look out for himself. Nothing that could be remotely compared to a tutorial or any oversight of any kind was in being. My results were never better than middle of the road.

It was during my time on the *Richmond* that I first began seriously to question whether the career I had set out on with such enthusiasm really was what I wanted. My days at sea were very happy ones, odd episodes apart. That was not what was bothering me. It had become clear in certain instances such as taking sights, or seeing distant lights on the horizon, that my eyesight was not as good as those around me. They could see things before I could, and take stars that I couldn't even locate. This was potentially serious, for when taking second mate's exam, the board set a very searching eye test at which glasses couldn't he worn. In the event, my fears were well grounded. Further, though marriage was to be some years down the line, I was in no doubt at all that I would marry—and the sea was not helpful to married men. In my day there was no provision for even captains to have their wives with them. And when later that did happen, it still didn't answer the problem of children. Finally, I had become aware that the marine side almost never graduated to a role in running the company at board level. There was however within me, the beginnings of a sense that I would want, ultimately, to be the deciding voice in whatever role finally emerged. That this would almost certainly entail being head of a mouse rather than tail of a lion didn't matter.

It was about this time during my last year of cadetship (I would be nineteen) that George offered me a post as a trainee journalist with the *Cape Times*. It sounded attractive, and I liked the country, though not unaware of the colour problem. However, I thanked him but declined. My concern at that stage was to complete my apprenticeship and get a 'ticket'. On the 10th December 1949 I came ashore, having got sufficient sea time to enable me to go forward for 2nd Mates. Liverpool had its own nautical college, which I attended from the New Year. It was a sort of crammers' course, designed to overcome a want of application over the previous three years! In May I took the exam and apparently satisfied the requirement.

All, that is, except the lifeboat certificate. This was a practical business conducted in one of the Liverpool docks by a retired M.N. captain, one Captain Vincent. It called for a demonstration of boat handling and knowledge. At the risk of immodesty, on both *Conway* and the *Gerusalemme*, I had had my full share of such. It was a cold day and our elderly examiner allowed his nose to run which seemed to me very distasteful. It might be I was unwise enough to let it show. Whatever the cause, he became very critical of my efforts, and took something fairly close to pleasure in failing me. Fortunately, these tests were held every couple of weeks and my next attempt was under a different man who passed me without difficulty. Perhaps I should have previously taken a course in dissimulation!

By early June 1950 I was the proud possessor of a brand new 2nd Mates Seagoing Certificate that to this day has never been used. Half a century later, an old friend from training ship days, one Reg. Kelso, who also joined Union Castle and became first a Captain, and then Chief Marine Superintendent, was saying how desperate companies were for officers with English certificates. Quoth I: "I shall offer myself, for I have such a qualification!" "Ah, no," returned he, "the need really isn't *that* great!"

At one time Reg. had command of a substantial passenger ship called the *Reina Del Mar*. As with all such boats there was a large complement of stewards. One such was a chap called John Prescott. This fellow had a bit of a reputation as a sea lawyer. (In the army they call them barrack room lawyers!) Either because of or despite this he became, and is, the Deputy Prime Minister!

During my study time I qualified for unemployment benefit, which my peers and I did not fail to collect. It was 130p a week (£1-6-0). The eye test was a trying time. I failed on my first attempt, but the examiner, who realised how much hung on the outcome, was very kind. He advised me to go home, rest my eyes in darkness, bathe them in boracic and come back—then return for a further attempt, at the end of which I suspect he gave me the benefit of the doubt. That decided me there and then to seek another way to earn my living, for that eye test would be repeated some years down the line for both Mates and Masters certificates, when the slightest further deterioration would end my career.

But that is another story.

THE COMMERCIAL WORLD

It was one thing to decide to quit a career, and one for which I had spent the last five years preparing. It was quite another to replace it with something which, hopefully, would have at least equal prospects. It seemed a sensible first step would be to talk to my father about joining the family business. His response was to tell me to talk to my uncle.

The company had been started at the turn of the century by one Jacob Atherton, son of the local squire, at a time when laundries were just beginning to be seen as a mechanised alternative to traditional ways of maintaining cleanliness. He lost interest once it was operating, and my grandfather agreed to buy it. What he used instead of money has never been clearly established—possibly some very extended payments arrangement! However, he became the sole owner, and moved to a small terraced house in Prescot from his previous, similarly terraced, home in Bolton. He had three sons, the eldest of whom was academic and won his way to a grammar school education. He rejected the laundry as a career out of hand, as offering no future. Neither the middle son (my uncle), nor my father, the youngest, was academically gifted, leaving school at the earliest possible date. Both went into the laundry business, my father graduating to firing the boiler, and uncle helping with the deliveries.

On my grandfather's death, the two brothers inherited the operation. Neither having been very impressed with their respective roles, they had started up a garage on some spare space at the front of the laundry. Cars were beginning to multiply, and servicing them was a coming business. My father had gained some engineering experience when he had served in the Royal Naval Air Service in the First World War. To this they added a taxi service, and formed a motorcycle club. For some years this enjoyed a modest prosperity, and there was even talk that it would take over from the laundry. In the meantime, the management of the laundry operation was left in the hands of a young operative of above average promise, and who had been promoted to manageress, a Miss Annie Lyon, later on (after marriage), Gerrard.

Then the Second World War began. Cars melted from English roads, whilst military demand for laundry services rocketed. The garage was reduced to a single

58

petrol pump and the laundry prospered. By 1950 the war was long over and the first stirrings of competition had begun to make themselves felt; easy wartime profits were no longer in evidence. The company began to lose money. Worse, plant had been installed earlier, to be paid for out of the profits of future trading, the interval bridged by bank borrowing. By 1950 the bank was getting restless, and was pressing for a reduction in an overdraft that had taken on a very permanent look.

This was the background when I went to meet my uncle. My request to be allowed to join the firm was dismissed, even though offering to work whatever hours it took for £5 a week (on returning to sea as a fourth officer, my salary would have been about double that). His response was that there was no money to pay anything. The legal structure of the company was that of an equal partnership—each brother owned 50%. Neither could take any course of action without the agreement of the other. Therefore my father could not allow me to join on his own initiative. This arrangement was to prove of the first importance later.

Returning from this abortive interview, my first action was to write to George Young in Capetown to enquire whether that post of trainee journalist was still available. Mail in those days was rather leisurely, even air mail taking ten or more days. Three or so weeks elapsed before a very positive response said: "Come!" Included was an invitation to stay initially with the Youngs whilst sorting out my own domestic arrangements. My place was to be in the shipping office at a starting salary of £26 a week. Riches indeed!

About ten days after that first, and unhelpful, discussion with my uncle, a message arrived via my father that he wished to see me. It later emerged that in the interval he had been talking to his brother-in-law, whose entrepreneurial skills he held in high esteem. The advice he had received was effectively, "Let the lad come, he might just do some good. If he doesn't, you are planning to close anyway, so the only downside would be a few weeks pay, at five pounds a week!" So it was that a start could be made the following Monday. My wages would be £5 a week and I would be an ordinary weekly paid employee with no legal status. He was honest enough to say he thought the job would last only a short period, as the partners were facing the inevitability of closure.

From having no job, I now had one and was shortly to receive an invitation to another! The positive response from South Africa was to put me on the spot. Not only was the money vastly better, it had a much more permanent look about it. Though not trained as a journalist, with the brash confidence of youth, I felt sure I could master the art. Though I never did become a journalist, my younger daughter certainly did! By the time the Young response arrived several days had already been spent at the laundry, and there was within me that which wanted to give it my best try. My decision was to do something that in today's world would be unthinkable. I wrote back and said that having secured a temporary job, would it be all right to keep in touch with a "view to taking up the offer at a later date?" Those were the days of full employment! The response, when it came, was favourable. In passing, it may perhaps be noted that correspondence with George began in 1947, at first, no doubt, mainly thank-you letters for hospitality received, etc. For the next sixty-five years, until his recent death, that correspondence continued.

Arriving promptly at 8-00 a.m., my uncle was there to greet me. This was a special favour; he didn't usually turn up until 9-00 a.m. I expected to be given some specific task, such as being seconded to someone to learn a role; but instead, having donned a carpenter's apron, my uncle said to follow him. He had a lump of putty and preceded to walk round various tables, some of which had recessed but exposed nail heads. Into these he placed some putty, assuring me as we went that if this wasn't done and there was any moisture about, iron stains could mark the clean linen. After about an hour of this, he told me to carry on and repaired to the little general office where he had a desk. It emerged that his two chief activities were smoothing used paper and collecting string which he knotted together and formed into a ball of disparate types, all for further use. When he ran out of string and paper, out would come the cash bag and the coins poured out onto the desk ready to count. This, it soon became obvious, was his favourite activity, which probably explained why it happened two or three times daily! He once told me that he had had ambitions to be a bank clerk. What he forgot to mention was that he had applied, but lacked the academic qualifications!

With my one hour 'induction' completed, I was obviously on my own. It quickly became clear that neither brother had the faintest idea of the basics of either the laundry world in particular, or managing a business in general. My father was able to keep the machinery going, and his older brother was in overall charge. Laundries aren't high tech. They offer a very basic service (though surprisingly important, in the war, laundry work was a reserved occupation). It didn't take long to master the rudiments. The business was run by the devotedly loyal, but now elderly manageress, Mrs Gerrard, well into her sixties and totally unresponsive to anything that was remotely new or involved change. Such knowledge and skills as she possessed, she guarded jealously from me on the grounds that my presence was a threat to her position.

Whilst seeking to understand the operation on the ground, contact had been made with the trade organisation to see what help might be forthcoming from that direction. There were two things they did for me which proved over the years to be hugely beneficial. One was to introduce me to costing and management accounting, the other to link me up with a Liverpool launderer who was, they said, at the cutting edge of the game. His name was Joe Skeaping who, together with his cousin, owned the Dexter Laundry. My uncle regarded a set of costing and account sheets, bought with my own money, a complete waste, and immediately set about reducing the company affairs to a profit and loss scenario. In the event it was only loss! But at least the scale of the task and the areas to he tackled became very clear. The one area that stuck out like a sore thumb was payroll. Joe and I became good friends, and he gave me all the help he could, despite my being at least a potential competitor. A couple of months into the job he offered to come and take a look at Prescot to see if he could offer any ideas. Having taken a good look round, he took me to one side and said, "The only advice I can possibly give is sell while there is something left to sell" This was not particularly encouraging, but was at least in line with the brothers insistence that they would have to close.

This is possibly the moment to look at some figures. In the year 1950 (which was when I joined, in July), the turnover averaged £189 a week (£9840 p.a.); but of this some £50 a week was petrol sales with a very modest mark up of some 6%–7%. By the time maintenance and licences were paid, there was no worthwhile profit from sales of fuel. This made us the smallest laundry on Merseyside. The two brothers were taking £20 a week each, not a king's ransom, but a huge percentage of the real turnover, some 28%! This might just have made sense if there was a significant input from them. My father did contribute a little through machinery maintenance, whereas my uncle's was barely measurable. In neither case was there going to be any change in this. For one thing, my father was pushing sixty.

There *was* an awareness of this problem, because from time to time my uncle would say "management charges will have to be reduced." Action, however, never followed! It was plain that far too many people were employed for the output. The top rate for a woman was £3 a week, though there were several youngsters; a fifteen-year-old started at about 14/-a week (70p). We were offering a quality service, and certainly had a price list to match, which simply meant there was very little scope for price increases. My resolve therefore was to reduce and simplify the various operations; this, however, met with rock solid opposition from the abovementioned and devotedly loyal manageress, Mrs Annie Gerrard! There was never any support from the brothers. My father could always sense trouble arising, and unfailingly responded by emigrating across the road to the pub, where he was always welcomed as the firm's best customer! My uncle would bluster and declare the matter had to be sorted, and then leave me to it. My secret weapon with Mrs. G. was, in extremis, to hint at retirement. This was usually enough to close the issue, with Mrs G. retreating and declaring that when the place had been wrecked, it would be no use trying to blame her.

Some jobs were eliminated simply by abolishing the task; for example, all shirts had been hand-scrubbed before being washed by machine—an excellent way of reducing the life of the article. The next step was to increase the productivity of the remainder. A logical and mechanised marking system that replaced pen and ink was a first move. This not only speeded the process, but made it easier for other than packers and sorters to do the job, and diminished the stranglehold they had previously held. The equipment for this was second-hand and involved a minimal capital outlay. It did not prevent a battle to get my Uncle Stan to agree.

The company had two small vans, an 8 h.p. and a 10 h.p. that collected and delivered the linen. The interval between the two was about thirteen days. That was the length of time it took to process the stuff. This was quite impossible—customers never got their work back on the same day and never knew when to expect it. Clearly, a high priority was to speed up the throughput in the factory to achieve a regular weekly delivery. This was easier said than done, for there was a great deal of inertia and no one wanted to change his or her ways. Even the two brothers saw the upheaval as a tiresome minus, overlooking the potential gains that could flow from it. Conveniently, one of the two van drivers fell sick and decided to retire, opening the way to selling the two small vans and replacing them with one slightly larger one.

It was during these moves that a deputation came to me to say the employees had it in mind to join a union. They were clearly worried about change, actual and prospective, and wanted to gauge my reaction. Having myself been a member of a union when at sea, no proper reason seemed to offer itself why others should not do likewise if they wished. Quite apart from which, the company belonged to a trade association, which by definition was a group of employers joined together to promote their shared economic interests. This, it must be supposed, is also what defines a trade union! So shortly after that there was a visit from the District Official of the Municipal and General Workers Union. We got along well. I had to be quite firm that we had to increase our efficiency and output very significantly, if we were to survive, and he was to have some members. There were advantages in having an experienced and knowledgeable union official to talk to. I was still very inexperienced, and he had a realistic understanding of the commercial world. If he could be persuaded of the need to do something in the longer-term interests of his members, he could explain the situation to them and secure co-operation more easily than might have been the case from myself.

All of this seemed to me a perfectly reasonable way to proceed, but word got round the industry that we were unionised and the floodgates opened. The laundry world at that time was made up of some 2,500 mainly small, family owned units. The owners were a fiercely independent group, with a visceral hatred of unions which they saw as enemies potentially cramping their style. Some members from the local trade association came to see me to deplore my selling of the pass, and urging action to remove the union. The London office of the trade association both rang and wrote to the effect that my actions were extremely damaging. Even my new friend, Joe Skeaping, was horrified. On pointing out to all in turn that we lived in a democracy, nobody could understand the link.

The M.G.W.U. remained, and I had to accept something close to pariah status among my peers. This was less onerous than might have been, for my attendance at Institute of British Launderers meetings was not frequent. At these gatherings there seemed to be much smallness of mind, and petty boasting of this or that achievement. One learnt not to ask a competitor how trade was, for unfailingly the answer would be hugely positive. Rather, I would lead in with how difficult we were finding things. With that preamble, sometimes it would result in getting something approaching the truth! Years later, my learning to live with unions was to produce a huge bonus, but that was not visible at the time.

Whilst the first twelve months was intensely busy on the factory floor, some time had been taken to look at our office procedures. Two ladies looked after the bookkeeping, telephoning, etc. The one in charge, a Miss O'Brien, was elderly and avoided the phone like the plague; she could never come to terms with it. So the junior had to cope. Occasionally, when she did have to grapple with it, her voice rose to an agitated crescendo akin to a semi-controlled scream! On one occasion, pressing for some clarification of a procedure, Miss O'Brien, unable to explain, said, "You see, we just sort of 'muddly' through!" Everything was done with pen and ink. There were no machines at all, save one enormously large and heavy typewriter, which had first seen the light of day not much after the turn of the century.

By this time an information flow, that enabled an accurate and reliable management account to be produced very promptly, had been established. Initially monthly, this quickly seemed too long an interval, and it became a weekly document. It was my compass, and I came to rely on it totally. Any cost deviance was quickly apparent, and could be tackled at once. There was a useful fall-out gain inasmuch as those supplying the information also began to take an informed interest in consumption and cost. Until my last week in the business, this P. & L. and management cost control system functioned perfectly. From time to time other information was added, always in response to a felt need. The most important, as capital expenditures increased, was a rolling twelve-month cashflow projection. This too, once established and updated monthly, continued to the end of my period of office. Balance sheets were of less concern. Whilst there are moments when they are vital, for the most part, if the company makes good profits, the balance sheet will look after itself. As more of the business became based on a system of monthly accounts, the debtor position was monitored very closely. The cheapest money any company can get is that which belongs to its suppliers! Holding on to invoices as long as possible is almost an art form!

After a couple of years, and looking for ways of involving our people more closely in the company, I thought to make the management accounts available to everybody, and accompanied by some notes. This would enable them to see exactly what was happening and why. Discussing this with Mr Welles, the union official and a much older man, he advised most strongly against it. He didn't think his members could be trusted with the information! Unions tend to be very conservative—with a small 'c'! Against my better judgement, I deferred to him. It was only several years later that it was decided to go ahead anyway, and I never had cause to regret doing so.

Though sufficient progress had been made to bring the business back into profit, and this had removed the pressure from the bank, it became increasingly clear that there was no long-term future in the one market we served, the domestic household. Too large a proportion of the charge was consumed on costs that didn't benefit the housewife. Collection and delivery cost was very high, and sorting, marking and packing costs were also substantial. None of these, however, were valued by the customer, who just wanted her sheet washed and ironed. It was time to look for other markets. The obvious one was to move into dry-cleaning. This, from the end of the Second World War, was a growth market. The downside was that it required a completely different set of machinery; laundry plant could not be adapted. Thus began a battle royal with Stanley to get his agreement to make the money available. My position in relation to him had strengthened considerably. The measures taken had been successful, albeit modestly, and he couldn't gainsay them, but they had all been achieved with no, or minimal, capital expenditure, and turnover was rising steadily. The cost however of moving into dry-cleaning couldn't be achieved at less than £1,500, and it would be a struggle to keep it to that figure. This was a sufficient sum to give Stanley nightmares.

The battle was finally won—space was made available, the plant installed, a shop frontage opened, a little advertising (not much, the budget didn't allow), staff trained, and we were in business. Prescot at that time had three competing dry-cleaning shops, but they were really only receiving depots. Their work had to go to a factory some miles away to be processed. We did it on the premises, a major plus. It had been decided also to opt for a white spirit plant rather than the increasingly popular 'triklone' alternative. It was less automated, but much kinder to the garments.

In a matter of weeks we had swept the board. Two competitors closed within months. Johnsons hung on. The company finances were transformed. Whereas the average unit price for a piece of laundry was about seven pence, for dry-cleaned work it was around four shillings, an almost 700% increase, whilst the labour involved was not significantly greater. In short order, half a dozen outlets were opened in surrounding shopping areas, and cleaning turnover quickly overtook the laundry side.

Before this, and within a year of my joining, my father was taken seriously ill. He was a heavy smoker, getting through fifty high tar cigarettes a day and inhaling every one. Not surprisingly, he got cancer in his throat, and was out of action for some eight months. He never opposed my ideas, but was never supportive either, so in terms of my wrestling with his brother it made little difference, and I had more or less mastered sufficient knowledge of the machines to be able to cope most of the time with breakdowns. Relations with Stanley deteriorated steadily as he proved an unending drag on almost everything that needed to be done. As the profitability continued to improve, his chief concern was to hold onto the money rather than put it back into the business. Mine could not have been more different. After one vigorous set to, he stabbed his finger at me and said, "Lad, if your father dies, you are out the next day!" As the firm was a partnership he could only sack me with his brother's consent, and that was a sticking point, even with my father. In the event my father recovered and lived for another decade.

Within a year of my father's return, Stanley was taken ill and was out of commission for several months. This gave him a problem. He realised that the continuing functioning of the company was effectively in my hands, but was scared to death of what I might do whilst his back was turned! In the event we continued to make steady progress. He was so relieved that on returning, he offered to buy a set of rather smart, chromium-plated horns for my car. This duly happened, but the goodwill effect wasn't helped when he threw a tantrum because the bill was a couple of pounds more than he had expected! It didn't help when, about a year later, the car was sold—complete with horns!

Both partners enjoyed their full salaries throughout their periods of sickness, as they were to do in subsequent absences. My own £5 a week stipend remained at that level until the large boost to profitability brought about by the dry-cleaning side. It was about this time that Stanley, almost certainly advised by his brother-in-law, took me to one side and said he thought it was time for me to have an increase. This was happy timing, for I had been on the point of raising the matter myself! He proposed an uplift to £5-10-0 a week, or 10%. My counter proposal was for £15 a week—in other words, an increase of 300%! His shock was profound, but when all I had to do was to point out it was a tiny fraction of what my efforts had delivered, he yielded. By this time my position was very strong, except legally. My status remained that of an hourly paid employee. In retrospect, perhaps this nettle should have been grasped sooner than when it finally was, in 1957. My father's share would come to me, and it hadn't seemed too important. Stanley had no heir to succeed him, and that would almost certainly mean he would want to be bought out. This in the event happened.

Every few months in the earliest days, Stanley would say, "Management charges will have to be reduced"—but that was as far as it ever got. After the dry-cleaning side kicked in, there was a period of silence. Then one day he suddenly said, "You know, management charges will have to be increased; they haven't been moved for years." It gave me a peevish pleasure reminding him just how often he had spoken of the need to reduce them! An adjustment was agreed nonetheless.

My conviction remained that there was no future in domestic laundry services. It was too labour intensive, and labour was plainly going to be a remorselessly increasing cost. In fact, there was an unfailing upward revision of pay rates every year. The obvious replacement was contract work. There were huge cost reductions available that more than offset the lower charges that applied. One van could collect from a single client in half a day, more work than its domestic counterpart could get in a week. Sorting and packing costs were dramatically reduced, as were office outlays. Contract work began to replace domestic, though the latter didn't finally disappear for several more years. We kept our charges for household work right at the top. At least, if we were going to do it at all, we would make something out of it.

About 1937. Caps were worn most of the time!

Second term 'Conway' boy. The stiffener had gone from my cap!

With my sister, after joining the merchant navy.

H.M.S. *Conway* in the Menai Straits.

Madras harbour, 1946. Coxing the ship's lifeboat.

The *Gerusalemme* in the Grand Canal, Venice, being returned to her
rightful owners!
Looking rather down at heel!

The girl I fell in love with! Judy graduating from Manchester University
With B.A. Hons. in English.

Our wedding day. Sept.20th 1958.

My home base for the first 28 years.

Our complete and growing family, circa 1980.

The house we built for our married life, after
it had been extended.

Len Murray, officials of the T & G Union, and myself, at home
before the official opening of the new factory.

The new factory shortly after completion.

A model of my largest single development, built on the site of the former Chorley Briggs laundry.

Anne, our elder daughter, about to be married, 1986.

Mandy, our younger daughter, ready to cross the road to the church in
the background, a few years after her sister.

The Old Rectory from the church tower opposite.

And in summer from the croquet lawn.

The only new R.R. I ever had, and kept for eighteen years!

An elderly, but much loved old lady. 1955 Silver Dawn.

Enjoying Hugh and Alice, a couple of grandchildren.

Nine of the eleven grandchildren, circa 1999.

It wasn't all work!

Judy, 2004.

A GIRL APPEARS

Returning to my first days after leaving the sea, I was in the front garden of my parent's semi, cutting the privet hedge. It was to become one of my regular chores. Looking up at two cyclists as they rode past, I found myself utterly smitten by the young girl. Her companion was a pimply youth of no great merit! Given she was on a bike meant she probably lived not too far away, and my resolve there and then was to find out where that was. My luck was in, for it turned out her home was on the same road, not more than a hundred yards away! Thus began my pursuit of the maiden, a pursuit that was to last all of seven years. No one should ever try and persuade me that there is no such thing as love at first sight. Judy, for she it was, was sixteen at the time and I was twenty. Having made contact, she accepted an invite to meet, and my world took on a whole new dimension.

Everything about that first shared occasion confirmed my utter conviction that this was the girl I wanted to, and would, marry. There was just one snag—she didn't share this view! Before parting, I had tried to arrange a subsequent meeting, only to be met with a polite, but very firm, "no". That extra dimension evaporated! In succeeding months I would think up all sorts of things that we might do together, only to have the majority turned down with unfailing courtesy. Just once in a while she would say "yes", and I would walk on air. These occasions were invariably enjoyable, though she kept me firmly at arm's length. Then each "yes" was followed by a further number of refusals, except when it was possible to be useful, such as running her to her university digs, for I had acquired a small, eleven year old, Hillman drophead coupe on leaving the sea. That Hillman, despite its age, cost me twice what it had when it was new! In part this was due to inflation, but more to the desperate shortage of cars of any sort in those early post-war days. No private cars had been built for about six years, and it took time for the factories to convert back to peacetime production—added to which a very high proportion had to be exported to help the balance of payments.

All is fair in love and war. This general pattern endured for about seven years, throughout which time my belief remained that she would become my wife. Looking back, perhaps it was for the best, though it didn't seem so at the time.

The business demanded a very large input of time and effort, into which an active courtship would have made significant inroads. In those seven years my total time on holiday wasn't more than a couple of weeks, a state of affairs that any girl worth her salt would not have been likely to tolerate! It shouldn't be thought that this lack of formal holidays was a minus. My work was absorbing, the challenge was stimulating, and I found it totally re-creative. So 'recreation' as such was not a high priority.

My grandfather had been a Freemason and Stanley had followed suit, but not my father. Prescot had just one branch, Lodge of Loyalty 86. This was thought to be quite prestigious. By Masonic standards it was very old, celebrating its two hundredth anniversary in 1951. So, pressure was put on me to join to maintain the family tradition, and this I did in 1950. It struck me at the time as being slightly odd that it was required of me to sign a document saying I was joining of my own free will, having not been subjected to any external persuasion! In fact it wasn't persuasion they subjected me to—it was more like bullying! The ceremonies, each heavily solemn, whereby the applicant was passed through the three 'degrees' to master mason, were, it seemed to me, rather silly, though quite harmless.

Having become a 'master mason', the next three lodge meetings were devoted to processing the next fellow, and the three after that another chap. It was about that point that I asked when we would be doing something useful. The response was—we were doing it! That, combined with execrable meals at the local hostelry after the meetings, and the even worse speeches delivered every time, brought my involvement to an end. My Masonic career lasted just a year. There are many who find in its arcane ways satisfaction and pleasure, and there was, of course, the social side always with the possibility that one might meet someone able to be helpful. Those with a feeling for theatre and drama were particularly likely to find it satisfying. For my own part there were other more pressing uses for my time.

During my year as a mason I got to know the tyler; he was the chap who, for a modest fee, opened up and got the lodge ready, and then stood guard whilst the meeting was in session, ready to repel any boarders! He had spent many years on the great North Atlantic liners, including the old *Mauritania* and the Queens, as a member of the ships' orchestras. I have forgotten what instrument he played, but with my own merchant navy background, I enjoyed chatting to him. His name was Dodd, and from time to time would mention his nephew who was making progress as a comedian in the entertainment world. The nephew was Ken Dodd!

I first came across Ken at the Exchange Hotel in Liverpool (long since pulled down). Once a year, the Liverpool branch of the Institute of British Launderers held a dinner dance that was well supported. Back in the early fifties there were a significant number of laundries. One year, I think it was probably 1951 or 1 952, Ken was engaged to do two 'spots' in the course of the function. There wasn't a lot of dancing that evening; he greatly overran his allotted time, and the whole gathering was just rolling in the aisles. Everyone was talking about this chap. The rest is history!

By about 1953 my position in the company had become almost unassailable. All the various steps to reduce the business to a profitable base had delivered steady incremental gains, and the move into dry-cleaning had proved a winner. Relations with Stanley continued to be strained but as a chief beneficiary of the gains of the recent past, he had begun to adopt a less defensive role. Only when large capital expenditure reared its head did he rouse himself to serious objections, and even then he invariably finished up yielding. It might be that his opposition served a fruitful purpose. Before coming up with the next plan, I made certain that everything in my power was done to ensure it would work. The one thing that would undermine my position would be getting a project wrong. In short order a new boiler house was built, and a new automatic feed boiler installed, though still coal-fired. It was much more efficient and so reduced coal bills, and labour costs.

The dry-cleaning side very quickly required larger plant as shops were opened in quick succession. At the peak we had about a dozen retail outlets, and half a dozen vans serving the dry-cleaning market. Space began to be a problem. A first move in this direction was to build up what had been the garage forecourt, the frontage of which formed two handsome shops, one for laundry and the other for dry-cleaning. Opposition from the usual source was softened by including a private office for the exclusive use of Stanley, who for once became really quite excited by the proposals!

It was the largest single piece of expenditure to date at over £3,000. But a private office—now *that* was something to be reckoned with! Stanley had always had a picture of himself as a high-powered executive. One of the first cost reductions after my arrival in 1950 had been the discovery of quarterly rental charges for an internal telephone system. This consisted of a phone on Stanley's desk linked to another about ten feet away and attached to a wall. This had been installed because Stanley thought it would look good to have a phone on his desk! It was never used because there was no scope for using it, and anyway it hadn't been intended to be actually used! When I was still at sea Stanley had asked me to get him some of the colourful labels issued by shipping companies for passengers to stick on their luggage. The idea was to put them on his cases, so when going on holiday it would look impressive to other guests! Perhaps, sadly, he never took an overseas holiday in his life.

By now the business had built up some momentum, and it became necessary to develop a strategy for the future. In part, this involved moving our position in the market place, but more, our internal organisation. What had become clear was that all the competition was using more or less similar machinery. There were no high tech. secrets or systems. Therefore, what would give one company a material advantage over others? The game was labour intensive, and payroll dom- inated our management account. My first pull at producing a management account a couple of months after arriving had shown some 70%+ of turnover taken by wages and salaries. Various measures had brought this down to less than 50%, but it was still far too high. It stood out very plainly that the company that could motivate its workforce and get them looking at things the way manage- ment had to, would lead the field. From this point on, much time, money and effort went into this objective, though it never seemed to me that real success crowned our efforts. A first step was to introduce a bonus scheme based on throughput, which was modestly successful in that it raised pay by about 10%– 15%, though it fell far short of my longer-term hopes.

All increases in turnover, at a time when inflation was minimal, involved addi- tional physical handling of linens and clothes, and pressure continued to build on available space. To the rear of the late nineteenth century brick-built factory were a number of wooden sheds and other low-grade ancillary stuff; these were cleared and two additional brick-built bays added. In 1950, nearly all machines were belt driven from a central gas engine. Progressively these were replaced with electri- cally powered equipment, the gas engine and housing removed, and the space made available for production. This represented the limit of the development potential of the site. Some time was bought by moving to larger machines. Equipment that would handle twice the volume took only a small amount of extra space.

From about 1953 I found myself having to live with the onset of arthritis at an uncommonly early age. It became progressively worse, so once a week for some eighteen months, I had some heat treatment at the local hospital. It became apparent that this was having no impact but was taking up time, so I abandoned it and decided it would just have to be lived with. Mornings were worst; it became necessary to get up half an hour earlier to get myself ready in time for work, because movement was so circumscribed and painful. This coincided with an increasing dissatisfaction with important aspects of my life.

These were centred in three key areas. After what seemed quite a long time there was no real progress in my relationship with Judy. Secondly, there was deep hostility towards Stanley. That he had made life very difficult, and my job of rescuing the company much harder than it need have been, was undoubtedly true, but in turn I had been pretty rough in response. Some, perhaps a lot, of the damage was down to me. I was not responsible for Stanley's actions, but was for my own. Lastly, the question of whether I should offer myself for the ministry had formed in my mind some time previously and refused to go away. But a large part of me wouldn't even consider it. The business held out the prospect of being reasonably prosperous, whereas the clergy were more modestly rewarded, at least materially—and I wanted to have some material success. The bottom line was simply that the ministry was not an option.

My normal practice was a short time of prayer in my bedroom before turning in. Then came this night when prayer was impossible; the three issues just mentioned dominated my mind, and I found myself engulfed in a state of black despair of a depth I had never experienced before (or since!). In that moment, from the innermost reaches of my being, there was a yielding of my own will. In silence I offered to do what my God wanted. Immediately some words of scripture sprang to mind, though it seemed to me as though they were spoken: "...if thou bring thy gift to the altar and there rememberest that thy brother hath aught against thee, leave there thy gift before the altar, and go thy way; first be reconciled to thy brother, and then come and offer thy gift." (Matt. 5: 23–24.) At once I knew my first task next morning would be to apologise to Stanley and agree a new working relationship that he would be comfortable with. I knew also that I would be able to do this, an action which just moments earlier would have been unthinkable and impossible.

Simultaneously, I found myself at peace over the question of progress with Judy. All sense of striving was ended, and a simple awareness that what was best would be. There was no feeling that my relationship, such as it then was, should end. Only that the straining be abandoned, and that I should stop trying to ordain predetermined ends.

Lastly, I knew at once and with an absolute certainty that it was not required of me to offer for the ministry. How? I hardly know how to answer, just that with utter clarity, as though the words had been spoken, I *knew*. The question has never touched me since. A couple of years later it was suggested I become a Reader in the C. of E. and it seemed right to take that step. With the benefit of hindsight it has become abundantly clear that I should have been a hopeless clergyman. Over the years my thinking has become steadily less and less orthodox, and more and more radical. As a Reader this hasn't been too important, but as ordained would have been very difficult.

Half a century ago there were many fewer Readers and in those days also all male. The small numbers and general lack of enthusiasm in the church at large for these hybrids was reflected in the manner of recruitment and admission. Any regular church member could offer himself, following which there was a short period of 'training' overseen by an already busy vicar. At the time I was an evangelical and my tutor a high churchman. My recollection is that we spent most of our time arguing the respective merits of these two wings of the church! There was an exam of sorts, though the barrier to entry must have been pretty low, for I was accepted. Not, however, without a comment to my own vicar by the chap in charge of the whole affair, one Canon Nelson. He declared, 'I don't think he knows very much about the C. of E., and what he knows he doesn't seem to like!" Sadly, Nelson later committed suicide, though I don't think my indifferent performance had anything to do with it!

Now fast approaching half a century, my years as a Reader have been on the whole interesting and fulfilling. Clergy divide quite firmly into two camps over Readers—some who can barely stand the sight of them, and others who see the possibilities of the office. Not every cleric is a gifted speaker, and perchance he finds himself with a Reader who is rather better equipped, that Reader may wait a long time before he is invited to address the congregation! But then not many of us like to be upstaged! Almost certainly, Readers will play a steadily greater role in the affairs of the church. The clergy are bent on maintaining their not insignificant compensation at a time when the finances of the church are increasingly stretched, indeed almost to breaking point. This has to mean, and indeed is already happening, a steady reduction in ordained numbers.

In a transforming second, from blackest despair in the deepest valley, I found myself on the mountaintops. The power and peace of that moment remain with me still half a century later, wholly undimmed. Life can't, of course, be spent on the mountaintops—the daily routines and ordinary demands remain, unchanged weaknesses and failings abound, mistakes and errors continue. All of that allowed, it was, and still is, the supreme and seminal moment of my life.

Immediately Stanley arrived in the office the next morning, my first action was to apologise for all and anything I had said or done that had hurt him, and I was ready to reach a new working arrangement. My recollection is that I didn't find it difficult to do. Stanley was taken aback, but sensed perhaps that we were at a watershed. He responded positively, and said he wanted me to continue to run the company. From that day on our relationship was a normal and positive one. We didn't, inevitably, always see eye to eye, but there are different ways of resolving such matters, and a different way was now in force.

The last word on this episode, the arthritis that had plagued me for the previous three years or so, quietly and quickly disappeared. Up to the present it has never reappeared. That there was a link between mind or spirit and matter in its onset, and again in its disappearance, is not in question for me. In due time, and without stress, my courtship of Judy bore fruit.

By late 1957 Judy, having given me quite some run for my money, gave indications that she was rethinking her response, and indeed we became engaged in February1958. We were returning from Lancaster. It was a cold, crisp evening with some snow on the ground. The sliding roof was open though the car was warm. I pulled into the side and popped the question. We both, I think, recognised that the time had come to get the matter resolved. Not surprisingly, therefore, the answer was "yes"! All of a sudden my status in the company became important. Having discussed it with Stanley, he decided that it was time for him to bow out. As mentioned earlier, he had no heir to follow and he was now well into his sixties.

The arrangement that emerged, after the usual bargaining, was that I would buy his entire share for £15,000. Given my pocket didn't have that sort of money, a deposit was paid and the balance bore interest on the reducing loan over ten years. This was all completed by the time of our engagement. Very shortly after Stanley's departure, the business was turned into a limited company with my father and self the two shareholders. At this time it was renamed. It had been called 'The Prescot Family Laundry Co.' in the days when long titles were fashionable. This became 'Cleggs of Prescot Ltd.'. When ultimately the company ceased to have a presence in Prescot, it became simply 'Cleggs Ltd.' In practice it had been known as 'Cleggs' anyway.

On reflection, all that had happened in the first seven years was to increase the amount that would have to he paid to Stanley on his departure. Was this wise? Something had to be done and quickly, if the company was going to survive, and there was no way a holding was going to be offered on day one. As my relations with Stanley deteriorated there was even less chance! Besides, there is little gain in speculating on 'what if?' In this world, you make your bed and lie on it. When we parted, it was in a friendly manner, and he would pop in quite frequently to see how things were going. Stanley had got a very full price for his interest. My gain was henceforth to have complete freedom to get on with the job. Both were happy with the outcome. To put values into perspective, our home in View Road, a year later, cost £6,000 to build, including the land. Probably a more arms-length price would have been about £7,500, Banny making an effective gift of the difference. His payout then was equal to two of those.

By this time my father was not a well man; the operation that had cured his cancer had been very painful and the effects protracted. The radium needles that had been inserted in his neck had almost destroyed his vocal cords, and for the rest of his life he could only whisper. This he found intensely frustrating, and made him unwontedly irritable. He chose not to retire when his brother went, and found enough things to keep him occupied, not excluding frequent visitations across the road! One moment of poignancy was coming across him in a corner smoking. Despite all he had suffered, nicotine still had him in its grip. He begged me not to tell my mother, so she never knew he had started again. Cancer returned, this time finally. After a prolonged fight, he just made it to his seventieth.

My recollection of him was of a kindly man who, as children, my sister and I could twist round our little fingers. If there were sanctions to be imposed, it was never my father, always my mother who chastised and corrected us. She was as strict as he was easy going. He loved to party and would be the life and soul, one reason he found the loss of his voice so hard to bear.

He delighted in practical jokes. At Christmas time one of the mince pies would have its content largely removed and replaced with cotton wool, the top then replaced. He would watch carefully to see who got it, and how the 'victim' coped before invariably spitting it out! Great hilarity all round! One time, however, the victim was a very shy, very polite chap. To my father's disbelief he chewed silently away and finished up swallowing it. He just wouldn't draw attention to himself. That ended the cotton wool mince pie episode. If that happened again someone might choke!

Another time he put an imitation spider in an aunt's Christmas dinner, hidden in the potato. When she came to it, there was a great shriek as she recoiled in horror, pushing her plate away as she did so. Once my father and the rest of us managed to stop laughing, he explained, whereupon aunt, in high dudgeon, left the table and refused to return. This cast a bit of a damper on the rest of the proceedings, and I don't recall any further spider escapades!

He also loved party games. A favourite was to send the victim out of the room whilst a chair with a string seat was prepared. This required a wet sponge placed on the seat over which a waterproof and cushion were placed and the whole of the bottom part of the chair covered to hide a metal bowl placed underneath. On being ushered back into the room the guest was asked what the last thing he or she did at night before going to bed. The one response no-one ever gave was to say they went to the loo! At that time polite people didn't discuss such matters. Finally, having been told every answer was wrong, they were asked to sit on the chair and think some more. The water from the sponge was immediately squeezed into the bowl beneath with very realistic accompanying acoustics! Gentle embarrassment on the part of the victim, and pitiless mirth indulged by the rest!

His great joys were cars and motorbikes, and I suspect that the days of the garage were the most fulfilling of his life. He was a very easy man to approach, friendly and outgoing, yet paradoxically, he and I were never close. There just didn't seem to be any common ground that we could share. He was happy for me to pursue whatever career or hobby I chose, but didn't follow its evolution with any interest. Nor did he try to involve me in anything that held his attention. In the whole of my life, including the years on training ship and at sea, I only ever received one letter from him. On being promoted to Senior Cadet Captain, my mother was so thrilled, she virtually forced him to write and say, "Well done." Very probably she stood at his elbow while he did so. It must have been painful—the result was just four, barely legible, lines. It might have been better had he not been pushed into advertising a limitation quite so visibly. Nevertheless, forgetting the plusses and the minuses in the way of a boy with his dad, I loved him.

About 1956 or thereabouts a meeting took place at the local vicar's house which was led by a Eugene Halliday, a man who was to have a strong impact on my life. At the time my outlook was essentially evangelical with all its narrowness and rigidity. As he spoke at that, and many subsequent gatherings which I attended, it became clear that he held, and was able to offer compelling grounds for a much broader and inclusive understanding of the nature and purpose of life. His mind had a quite extraordinary range, far beyond anything I had ever come across, either before or since. There seemed to be nothing that he didn't understand, or which he couldn't integrate into the totality of things. It was mind-stretching stuff.

He never sought to change anyone's opinions or ideas—all he did was to ask questions. But they tended to be ones that couldn't be answered from within the existing belief structure of the party concerned. This required that either one had to pretend the question hadn't been put, or to modify one's position to accommodate it. And so began the opening of my mind to a sense of the wholeness of life, of an undivided source of all, of its interlocking character, and ultimately its unity. Sectarian and denominational exclusivity evaporated. It was breathtaking stuff, the influence and ongoing evolution of which remains.

One element of his thinking that struck a chord was his assertion that the use of language fell into two categories. It could be used either 'actively' or 'passively'. By 'active' he meant having a clear and precise understanding of the value and context of the words being used. 'Passive' use was, of course, the opposite. In a debate, the former would invariably carry the day. Over the years I have found it to be wise counsel.

Becoming engaged brought a huge impetus to my life. That sixteen-year-old girl on her bike was, almost eight years later, to become my wife, as indeed I had believed she would—but this brought new responsibilities. A home had to he found, a wedding to be arranged and all the various new costs that come with such a relationship. Judy, of course, introduced me to her family and there I found immediate rapport with Banny Lucas who had married Judy's mum. 'Banny' was an abbreviation of Bannerman, after the Liberal prime minister of that name, his father having been a passionate Liberal supporter. He was a builder and we agreed that he would build a house for us if a plot of land could be found. Looking around, I came across a piece about a third of an acre in View Road, Rainhill. The owner wanted £800, which left me rather stunned. At that precise moment my home, with my parents, was in a well built, three bedroom, semi-detached with garden back and front and which had cost just on £1,000. And here was the vendor asking almost that—just for a bare piece of land without a brick laid.

Talking to Banny, he encouraged me, promising that if, having bought it, it was decided not to proceed, he would buy it from me for £900! It was bought, and he built a handsome four bedroom, cottage style house. Both Judy and I have always liked things old, but such were thin on the ground in Rainhill. What Banny built for us was the next best thing. He let me have it at a price that allowed me to borrow all of the capital, thus leaving something left over for carpets and curtains, etc. This was to prove the only occasion in the whole of my commercial career when I received what, in effect, was some financial help as a gift. It wasn't farsightedness, but the mortgage was arranged not with the more usual building society, but through the insurance broker who acted for the company, and had recommended an insurance policy with interest fixed for the 25-year life of the arrangement at about 4%. There were to be times during those 25 years when interest on building society borrowing reached more than four times that amount. Inflation peaked at 27% during Harold Wilson's government. Borrowing long in those years made much sense. Pounds were borrowed but, courtesy of inflation, effectively, pence were repaid.

Back at work there was much to be done. Turnover was now about five times the level it had been in 1950, and this represented almost a similar volume increase. Inflation in those far off days was running at only a couple of percent a year. Space was becoming critical, when onto the market came the next-door premises that faced onto the road to the rear of the laundry. It had been an undertaking business, and was of wood construction in a semi-derelict state. This meant we got it cheaply, demolished it, and built a two-story block. Offices and other ancillary needs were relocated upstairs, releasing space on the ground floor as well as the new area of ground floor made available by the new building. Demolition revealed that there was a difference in floor height between the two buildings of about two feet, which had to be dealt with by a ramp and, for heavy trucks, a lift. In the meantime the boiler had been converted to oil. It was a joy to have a clean boiler house and everything automated. I remember thinking that was the last we should ever see of coal. Little was it known at that moment that the clock would come full circle, but that lay in the future. Sometime later a second boiler was installed as the load increased.

We were by this time moving as rapidly as possible into contract work and were successful in winning some substantial orders, domestic work by now being confined to such as came in through the small chain of receiving shops. For the first time, the need was felt of a sales manager to hunt the business, and maintain links with the client once won. Other key personnel had also been recruited, a maintenance engineer and a production manager among them. These enabled me to spend more time trying to give an orderly growth and direction to the business.

As we entered the 1960's there were clear indications that the boom in dry-cleaning was over. Many had been attracted by the profit margins, and easy care fabrics were coming onto the market, added to which a more casual style of clothing was proving popular, but which required far less upkeep. All this conspired to trim margins substantially. Wages kept on rising and so the process of starting to close the least profitable shops began. The margins on contract work, whilst far better than domestic, were not in the same category as dry-cleaning in the glory days. It was time to find a fresh market.

For some time we had been working with a company that made work wear. They supplied the garments, and we were contracted to service them. It didn't take long to realise that here was the market we were looking for. The advantages of supplying the garments and servicing them on a binding contract were enormous. Once signed up, and subject only to providing a satisfactory service and the client remaining solvent, there was a guaranteed income, fifty-two weeks a year. An ordinary contract just servicing, meant you got paid only for what was received. But, there was a downside. There is no equity in boiler suits, so all purchases had to be for cash. And our cash resources were stretched. My uncle's loan was being repaid, my father's income was being met in full, though his input by this time was virtually nil. Marriage had brought its own set of new expenditures including mortgage payments, relatively large sums were being spent on buildings, whilst machines, either renewal or additions, were continuously ongoing. And dry-cleaning profits were turning down. The policy henceforward was to hoard cash for garments, and for everything else, if possible, to use borrowed money. It inevitably meant a fairly slow entry into this best of all markets. But at least our priorities were clearly established, and the desired direction set. A close look had been taken at the flatwork rental market, but it offered much poorer returns. It was very easy to do and there was much competition. A garment service required higher capital investment, and was much more complex to organise. Competition was far less.

Seeking long-term loans to speed progress came up against Stanley's prior charge on the business. Mainstream lenders don't like playing second fiddle. So a major effort was made to clear this as rapidly as possible, and we quickly reached a point where only a small part of any new loan would he used to discharge the remaining borrowing. The cash thus generated was welcome and helpful, and it was Eagle Star who provided the new funds. We also had a working overdraft, but in those days the clearers were not too excited about locking up their money for fifteen years or more, so they were not in the running for the sort of money we got from the insurer. All the monies we borrowed were fully secured, and as soon as some equity appeared in View Road, that too was used to provide security, and our home was on the line to the day the business was sold.

During this time continuing thought was given to motivating our people. One innovation was to provide interest free loans to help them buy their homes rather than rent. Laundry workers were somewhere near the bottom of the social heap and rates of pay reflected this (they still are and they still do!); putting money aside to fund a deposit was therefore very difficult, and where attempted, by the time a sum had been got together, inflation, which had begun to gather speed, meant it wasn't enough. We also undertook to give whatever help was sought in dealing with agents, solicitors, etc. The first occasion was a young man in the washhouse who was planning to get married. I remember talking to Tommy like a Dutch uncle, setting out how much rent he could expect to pay over a lifetime, with not a brick his at the end, and how much buying his home would cost, with a valuable asset at the end. He asked to bring his father in on the discussion, and I recall his dad's opening pitch: "Our sort don't buy, we rent!" With promises that if, after a period, he was unhappy with buying, the company would take it back off him at a price that would ensure he was not at a loss in any shape or form. On that basis he agreed to have a go.

Within a year he was chuckling that a house similar to his had just been sold for a hundred pounds more than he had paid. My recollection is that the price was about £1,000. To the best of my knowledge he is still in it. His mortgage will have been long paid off, and its current value probably around £100,000, possibly more. It didn't take long for others to come forward, with no persuasion at all needed! Over the years we were able to ensure that all our youngsters, ready to set up home, bought rather than rented. There was no security for our loans, but we never had a bad debt. Even where the party left the company with some loan outstanding, repayment was always made in full. The impact of this was very good for morale, and reached well beyond just those who were able to take advantage of the scheme.

Encouragement was given to open bank accounts. We offered to pay all bank charges up to a given sum, where the party agreed to have their money transferred direct to their account. This got off to a slow start, but gradually people came to recognise the benefits that could be obtained from an account. We introduced fully paid leave of absence where bereavement occurred, though quickly had to define the categories of relationship that qualified! One enterprising van driver applied for leave because his mother had died. He forgot that he had been given time off to bury her the previous year! A works council was formed, initially made up of charge hands and management, which quite quickly evolved to include shop stewards from the factory floor. To begin with, meetings were somewhat stilted. In the sixties not too many managements wanted to have the views and ideas of their workforces, and it took time for people to start to express themselves freely. It became over the years a valued vehicle of two-way communication, and there was quite lively interest in the elections.

It was somewhere around the mid-sixties that I felt we had made enough progress to share all the information that management had, and which informed their decision making, with our employees, and which demonstrated that they could be trusted not to abuse such knowledge. So the same management accounts were made available to everyone in the company on a weekly basis, together with a one-page report on developments during that week, and together with an explanation, where necessary, why profit was up or down. This was a welcome move, though in practice many took their lead from the relative few who had grasped what it was all about, and its relevance to their working lives. It was very much a case with many that 'If Sally says it's all right, it must be'. We had had two or three bonus schemes over the years but, like so many others, they were ad hoc and finished up being consolidated into the basic rate. A lot of time and effort went into studying what others were doing, and it was to be some time before we finally settled on a scheme which really worked, and which remained until my departure. But that still lay in the future.

MARRIAGE, HOME AND FAMILY

Judy and I were wed on 20th September 1958. She was 23, with her 24th birthday taking place whilst on our honeymoon, and I was 28. That young teenager on her bike, after a somewhat winding path, had become my wife. I loved her that first day I saw her, and I love her still. The honeymoon lasted a fortnight, substantially my longest break since leaving the sea. Female influence was already at work! From here on we did take regular annual holidays, though Judy would sometimes complain that all my employees had more time off than me!

The house was completed early in 1959, and we moved in with all the excitement of setting up home. The small front garden was quickly reduced to order. The back had to wait a while for funds to accumulate. Inside, carpets and curtains, together with enough furniture to get by, were soon installed. A new baby grand 'Welmar' piano, the product of three years saving, had been bought in 1953, and that helped to fill out the lounge. This was to continue in office for the next forty or so years when it was exchanged for a German built 'Steinway'. (The German pianos have a better reputation than the American version). An ambition fulfilled. It is a lovely instrument—pity about the pianist!

At the outset there were four bedrooms, but just Judy and I to fill them! We decided therefore to link up with a small organisation called 'The East West Friendship Council'. This was hardly more than a clearinghouse bringing students from overseas into contact with U.K. residents. Thus began a series of young people from many parts of the world staying with us for a part of their holidays. The very fact that they were over here studying at some of our best universities, meant they were of the elite of their respective countries. All were male, which said something about the patriarchal societies from which they came. The larger number were Muslim, though with one or two Hindus and Buddhists.

Apart from learning a little of their local customs and practices, we also brushed up on our geography. One youth came from Baluchistan. Having never even heard of the place, it had to be checked out in an atlas! The chief value for me was to begin a further stage in the broadening of my religious outlook. It was clear that for all of them their faith was a vital part of their lives, providing a foundation and a frame for daily life. Being alongside such, it just wasn't possible to dismiss these faiths as inadequate or, even worse, wrong. This argued for a closer look at just what their beliefs were. It became clear that they shared a vast amount of the truth that informs the Christian faith, and that the God they worshipped was the same God that Christians also worship. The labels and language may differ, but the truth is common. It may be yet some distance away, but the day will come when each will freely acknowledge the truth the other has. And the truth is undivided.

Within six months of our arrival in our new home, Judy bore our first child. Mark was several weeks ahead of schedule, and I had believed that when taking Judy to the hospital that night, it was a false alarm. It wasn't. My phone call to the hospital next morning, ostensibly to arrange to bring her home, was to learn that mother and son were both fine! It was one of the most moving moments of my life, and I could hardly wait to get to the hospital. Judy was in bed looking remarkably well and relaxed and holding our five pounds and some ounces son. Words do not easily do justice to such moments. A first need was to tell our immediate families. When it came to my mother, she said nothing till she had visibly counted off the months on her fingers; on arriving at ten, she broke into a wide smile and said, "How wonderful!" My comment to Judy later was that it was perhaps as well we hadn't rung a bell on the first night, or else my mother would only have counted to eight!

Just over a year later Anne arrived, more or less on time. She was born at home and I was therefore able to be present, again a most moving experience. I had been warned not to get in the way, and did little beyond holding Judy's hand. The average male tends to be a rather helpless creature in these situations. The midwife's view of a husband being present seemed to be that he had caused enough damage already without compounding it in the delivery room! Relatives were informed again, my mother's reaction being that it was a bit hasty, but then she decided that we had got our duty to the world over quickly by reproducing ourselves, and life could settle down from here on. With the third and fourth she just gave up on us!

It was about this time that I became involved with a young organisation called 'The Samaritans'. An Anglican clergyman, the Rev. Chad Varah, whose parish was St Stephen's, Wallbrook, in London, identified a need that wasn't being met. Many people are too shy or reticent to go to someone to seek help, especially if the issue is a very sensitive or personal one. Instead they soldier on until something gives, and they take their lives. It was Chad's idea to open a dedicated telephone line where a person could talk to an understanding and non-judgmental party, and share their difficulty without having to identify themselves. The idea took off. Liverpool became the next city to open a branch and in a very few years the idea had spread across the world.

Keith Lightfoot, who had earlier been a curate at Rainhill and with whom I had become good friends, had moved to the parish church in Liverpool. One day he rang to say "come and help." That began an association that lasted some fifteen years, the last several as its branch chairman. The whole thing involved a pretty steep learning curve, and the learning was about people. All of us get it wrong some of the time, but the law of averages dictates not all the time. There were folk, who as one listened to their problems, had clearly defeated the law of averages. They were men and women of all ages, social groups, income categories, sexual orientation and religious beliefs.

Also, it was a lesson in the art of listening. One call came through at about 2-00 a.m. That began an hour-plus monologue during which I spoke hardly a dozen words, just the odd interjection acknowledging I was still there! At the end the party finally drew to a close with the words, "Thanks, you have been so helpful!" Silence can be golden!

Was it successful in its prime objective of trying to help people through situations that had brought them to the verge of suicide? Only the failures could be measured—those who went on, despite Samaritans, to take their lives. Those that didn't might not have been going to anyway! It was for me a valuable episode in my life, until the time came to move on.

Whilst events at home were fast moving and enlarging the lives of us both, the business still demanded a great deal of time and effort. With two babes in quick succession, Judy had her hands full, though I did provide her with a full time daily help. Also, all the laundry, not surprisingly, was taken care of. This was supplemented by a daily nappy service which Mrs Gerrard latched onto and handled herself. By this time she was into her seventies, but totally unwilling to retire; indeed, she once said to me, "If you make me go, you will kill me." She wasn't made to go; she just pottered about doing her 'specials' until past eighty when she fell, mercifully at home, and died shortly after. It was that experience that made me introduce a compulsory retirement age of sixty-five.

It was shortly after the arrival of Anne that Judy got her first car. This meant we needed a second garage, though it had to wait for some time. When we did get round to it, a playroom, separate from the house, was also added. This was a place where the children could let their hair down and be themselves. In the house they were expected to behave in a reasonably civilised fashion.

Richard was next on the scene, this time with a little over two years interval. Again he was born at home, and again it was my great privilege to be present at his birth, my contribution once more being limited to holding Judy's hand and gently encouraging her. Giving birth is something the male of the species can barely relate to. He is not able himself to do so, and struggles to understand the impact, both physically and mentally, on the woman. Only, he must stand in awe of the demands it makes on a woman.

One of the areas we had discussed before marrying was the education of any children we might have. We both viewed developments in the state sector of education with less than enthusiasm, but agreed it would be my decision for any boys, and Judy for any girls we might have, and that education would have the highest priority in our budget. Education is a bird in flight—it must be shot on the wing! Cars, carpets. curtains, can all be bought whenever circumstances allow, but education is dictated by the growth of the child. As soon therefore as Mark was born, his name was put down for Mostyn House Prep. School and subsequently for Rugby, and likewise for Richard. Rugby accepted both, subject to the usual academic requirements, etc. When entering Mark, about a fortnight after he was born, I requested School House. The reply was that School House was full for many years ahead and it would be necessary to select an alternative. This left me wondering just how many years before the birth of the child was one expected to book! Judy wanted the girls to be educated in the private sector, but not as boarders. Accordingly they went to public day schools in Liverpool.

Later, when Rugby began taking girls for 'A' levels, Judy agreed that if Anne freely chose to go, she could. Anne's response was an immediate, one word reply—"Yes!" That she found her time there enjoyable would perhaps be an understatement. That she found the academic side commanding the same level of enthusiasm may not necessarily have been the case! Mandy in turn also said "yes" though she did not, I think, find her time there quite so rewarding. Only years later did it emerge, though it wasn't shared with us at the time, that because her three siblings had been to the school, she believed she was expected to go also. This was rather a shame, since our intention was that she should have the same unfettered choice, to go or not, as was the case with her sister.

Education is a very vexed issue in the U.K. The nation has some of the best schools in the world and also world-class universities. Students from all over the planet make their way here in testimony of this fact, and do so at very considerable cost. Tragically, we also have some of the worst that are routinely turning out youngsters who are functionally illiterate after a dozen years of 'education'. Current figures suggest that about one in seven, around 15%, fall into this category. These schools are concentrated wholly in the state sector and are the reason why, when international comparisons are made, the U.K. comes close to the bottom. There are one or two very basic reasons for this. The state sector is the ideological football of politicians who for sixty years have not hesitated to impose their 'principles' and push their 'reforms'. State sector education will never reach a satisfactory level until governments begin to see schools as institutions of learning, rather than as vehicles for social engineering. The other fundamental need is to restore discipline in school, and for this teachers must be given back meaningful sanctions. Every single school day in the year there are literally many thousands of children on the streets playing truant, with parents seemingly indifferent, teachers powerless, and government complacent.

Mark began to board at Mostyn House in September 1967, having spent, as all the children subsequently did, the first three years at the local church school at the bottom of the road, and where they got an excellent grounding in all the key subjects. The fees at Mostyn in those far off days were £137 a term plus the usual extras! Mandy's last term at Rugby in 1985 was about £2,000. Inflation since then is 100+%, so subsequent school fees have outstripped even inflation by a good 50% or more. But such is the condition of much state education that the public schools are full, and the demand even increasing, despite the very real sacrifices many parents have to make.

Those state schools that are up to standard, and there are some quite outstanding ones, do in practice involve the parent in substantial cost. Because the demand for places is so intense, they have had to limit their intake to defined areas. Within these the price of housing is higher by many thousands of pounds as parents move to be within range.

Finally, Mandy arrived about four and a half years after Richard—the gap getting noticeably longer with each subsequent arrival! With Mandy we called it a day. Earlier, when engaged, we discussed numbers of children and thought that six would be about right! Judy would certainly have had two more, but my concern was my ability to fund the cost of education. I also had to reckon with the fact that financially I was on my own—there was no possibility whatever of any fiscal help from either my or Judy's family. Events bore this out. We were, however, totally committed to the private sector, and obviously what was done for one must be done for all, so four it was. Do I regret putting the blocks on at four? In retrospect, "yes". The four have turned out so splendidly, all so different, yet all blessed with an abundance of commonsense, sound values, and a zest for life. Is it possible to have too many such?

Inevitably, decisions are made in the light of the circumstances of the moment, and the consequences of all decisions must be accepted.

We hadn't been married very long when Judy's grandfather died and the question of her grandmother's future was raised. Her then home was a large Victorian semi and manifestly too much for her to look after. She had four children, one of whom was to die quite shortly and prematurely. The remaining three didn't want to know when it came to providing shelter for her. All had reasons that may, or may not, have been adequate. Judy felt a debt of gratitude for the very committed help her grandparents had given towards her upbringing, and so it was agreed her grandmother would come and live with us, though by this time we had three children. A bedroom and the morning room were made available for her exclusive use and it was decided that she and we would live our own separate lives, at least as far as was reasonably practicable in a single home. She was a dear lady, but not unwilling to involve herself in the affairs of others, given any opening to do so. In due time alternative arrangements were made, and it was not unpleasant to have our home to ourselves once more.

GROWING COMMERCIALLY

As the company moved through the sixties, and towards the latter end of them, inflation became a serious problem. Wage claims were the root cause, and as a labour intensive industry, laundries were badly affected. Wages rose faster than customers could be persuaded to accept increased charges. The cry was '10% of nothing is nothing' so 20%, 30%, 40%, even 50% demands were made. No one seemed to notice that if 10% of nothing was nothing, so was 50%! Logic however is not usually the strongest suit in such affairs! As inflation moved over 20% and passed 25% we were reprinting price lists every three months. Large clients we talked to—our case was simple. If they wanted our service, and indeed anybody else's who was going to survive, there was no option but to seek increases that would match our outgoings. On the whole this was accepted, but much time and effort was consumed in countering the effects of inflation at these levels.

Laundry closures, and there had been steady net losses through the fifties, became a flood. One thing domestic laundries had to reckon with was the fact that the housewife, particularly with the advent of labour-saving home washing machines, was a serious competitor. Those with a large domestic element in their turnover were the earliest and chief victims.

During this period further moves to improve our internal operation were taking place. As in just about every other company (Mars, the confectioners, were an exception) our blue-collar people clocked on and off, our white collars didn't. This began to be seen as divisive; earlier it had just been accepted without query. Now the question was 'why?' Discussing this with my office manageress, she made a very strong argument in favour of retaining the clock, based on simple efficiency criteria. In my book, anything that contributed to efficiency was not to be compromised, still less to be lost. How to remove the divisiveness without losing the efficiency? We copied Mars. All would clock on and off, including myself. This last robbed the white collars of all real grounds for objecting. I clocked on until my last day from this time on—as did we all.

The key sectors in the company were each headed by a manager—production, sales, transport, office, engineering. The pressures of the job often made it difficult to pull a manager from his immediate duties, so I began lunchtime meetings with a different manager each day. For each there was a basic agenda, plus other relevant matters as they arose. To help compensate for working their lunch, the company paid for the food! These proved very helpful and enabled me to keep very close and continuing tabs on all that was happening in the business. They remained throughout my period of office. By this time, having long become accustomed to an inadequate memory, I had developed a simple system of reducing to writing all matters outstanding for each manager, including the date the matter was first raised, and removing them only when dealt with. This had the useful side effect that my managers came quickly to realise that nothing that was to their charge was going to be forgotten. It might as well therefore be done.

Lunch break had originally been one hour, with a ten-minute tea break morning and afternoon. Through the works committee this was negotiated down to, firstly, forty-five minutes, then to half an hour. The tea breaks were eliminated completely. In exchange, the working day was shortened by a comparable amount, and subsidised drinks could be taken from a machine as often as wished, taken back to the worksite, and the job continued. The overall effect of this was to shorten the time spent at work by almost an hour a day which, given 60% of our payroll was female, was a large gain for them. (My experience was that for the most part men wanted overtime, women didn't.) It also meant each individual could select from a choice of drinks when it suited, rather than having no choice at a regimented time. For the company the gain was considerable. Canteen facilities were upstairs, so at least five minutes was lost in 'travel' time at each end of each break. That added up to 100 minutes per employee per week. Shortening the week meant also a useful saving in fuel.

This period of high inflation, combined with recession, was to prove extremely difficult to negotiate. The company was locked into a large number of commitments that never seemed to reduce, only expand. There were not only the capital expenditures that were ongoing, most of which were essential for the continued growth of the business, but following my fathers death, the company had to pay the estate duties. Further, my father's will called for a £3,000 fund to be established for my sister, the interest on which was to go to my mother during her lifetime, and the capital sum to Ghreta on our mum's death. My father had made no provision of any sort for my mother on his likely prior death (he was ten years older than she), so that was a further demand on the company and which endured, with periodic adjustment, for the next twenty-five years. With rising inflation, so also interest rates increased, and the company was at all times a borrower. Some of those borrowings were at fixed rates, but not by any means all. By the late sixties we were struggling and extending our credit wherever possible.

In 1968 Mark had already started at Mostyn House. It was a Sunday and I was waiting for him to come out of chapel to take him home for the day. Another parent was similarly waiting and came over. It emerged that he held a senior position with Hogg Robinson, and one of his clients was Richard Baxendale Ltd., a substantial engineering business based at Bamber Bridge near Preston. They were later to become famous for their Baxi Bermuda central heating systems. The M.D. of the company, one Philip Baxendale, had asked him if he could find a buyer for two laundries which had come into the family by marriage, but which were not a fit for their core business. One was in Chorley, the other Blackpool. Following one of my golden rules, 'never say "no" on day one' on being asked "are they of interest?", my reply was a simple "yes".

Checking them out, it quickly became clear that Blackpool was a non-starter. A large proportion of the work was flatwork for boarding houses and hotels. Not only was it highly seasonal, as clients they were notoriously bad payers. Chorley was a very different cup of tea—chiefly contract work, exactly the stuff we were looking for; indeed, several of their clients, such as Heinz, we had repeatedly tried to win. They owned a detached house with vacant possession, and also a couple of receiving depots. Not only that, the plant had largely been renewed, with state of the art equipment in an unsuccessful attempt to make it profitable. The buildings, whilst in good repair, were, like so many laundries, our own included, old and not readily saleable in an area where cotton mills were closing, and low-grade industrial space was a drag on the market. The whole site was about two acres. The boiler was coal fired and had a hundred foot chimney which periodically belched smoke over new, high quality residential developments. The asking price was £50,000. The struggle began to find the cash to complete this unbelievably attractive deal.

My first call was Nat. West, our long time clearers. I had been supplied with Chorley figures, and these had been passed to the bank manager, and I also gave him a copy of my proposed plan. When we met he shook his head, said they were bigger than us, we had never attempted anything like this before, and a reverse takeover was not the way to begin—this at a time when I was not experienced enough to know that if the manager said "no", the next step was to ask for a meeting with his boss, the Area Director. Though the bank said "no" and, knowing no better, this had to be accepted, it was to prove important later that they knew they had been my first port of call. It didn't help when my accountants also thought the move an unwise one, asking rather pointedly what I knew that the vendors didn't, and whether I seriously thought that if there was money to be made out of the deal, Baxendales wouldn't want to make it for themselves? Well, I imagined I knew a little bit about laundries!

Casting around for anywhere that could provide the cash, David Oakes, an old friend from years back, proved to be the key that unlocked the door. He was the sort of chap who put himself about, met people, and so made himself the middleman. He undertook to talk to someone at Hambros whom he knew. They said the deal was too small for them, but knew of a small bank that had recently been set up as an offshoot of a firm of spice importers called J.H.Vavasseur. This bank was called the Vavasseur Trust. They were interested, the size of the deal being just right for them. Meeting their M.D., we went to look at the site and he agreed on the spot to fund the purchase. This was a straight loan, albeit with stiff interest, and the whole repayable in six months. Lawyers got to work, and the purchase completed with few complications. Baxendales were a company of high probity, and agreed readily to all the reasonable safeguards we asked for, such as guaranteeing the debtors.

One of my first tasks was to speak to the workforce, which was done at the end of the first week, to advise that the company was making substantial losses, which it was, and that it was not a viable operation; also making the point that it was a chief reason the parent company had sold, no doubt wanting to avoid the obloquy of closing it. This was accepted philosophically; jobs in the area were plentiful, and many qualified for redundancy payments. By the end of the first day, agents had been instructed to market both the shops and the detached house. Within a week I had located an architect and had arranged a meeting with the local authority planning department. This confirmed what had been fairly obvious. The business was a nonconforming user, but of sufficiently long establishment to be outside the power of the authority to get rid of it. Here was the owner offering, in exchange for a generous consent, to get rid of it for them. No more smoking chimney and complaining residents. We were welcomed with open arms. In short order, a planning consent for seventy-two flats was granted. By this time the plant had been closed, the work we didn't want sold on, and all the best contracts transferred to Prescot, including Heinz. Some plum pieces of machinery also found their way to Prescot, and the rest sold on.

The various properties didn't take long to sell. Well within the six-month deadline eighty percent of the cash had been returned to the bank. From the outset my relationship with Vavasseur hadn't been seen as a one off, but as the start of a long-term link that could be applied to many more acquisitions. For this reason my cap was set at being the ideal client. One thing had become obvious about lenders. They love good news, can cope with bad news, but hate silence.

My practice from the outset with Vavasseur was to write a weekly progress report to their M.D. In the way of these things nothing was said about this, but the sense was clear nonetheless that they loved it. Immediately on getting planning consent, Lavery, the M.D., was advised and told the agents would be instructed to sell the land forthwith. The bank would have all its cash back and interest paid well within the stipulated time and Cleggs would enjoy a fat profit. Oakes got his £10k finder's fee. Lavery's response was, "Why sell, why not build—we will finance you?" Fools rush in…The challenge was exciting.

Given the very limited building work that I had overseen up to that point, the wisdom of my decision to take on board overall responsibility for the building of a seventy-two flat development, might be thought open to discussion. However, Cleggs was once again on a sound footing; it had gained many thousands of pounds worth of top rate equipment free, which meant a considerable easing for a period of its own capital investment programme. It had enjoyed a large influx of first class contract work from blue chip customers, which worked wonders for the bottom line. Chorley rescued Cleggs from a situation that was calling our survival into question.

There were other useful gains—all their consumable stores were transferred to Prescot. These were quite considerable, and proved an ideal way to get our suppliers' credit back to normal levels! This gave me the idea of going to auctions of bankrupt laundries. Invariably there were stores, but for some reason no one seemed very interested, so we bought the lot for a tiny fraction of their value. Many times we returned from a sale with a couple of vans loaded to the limit with several tons of stuff. Some very useful savings were obtained, until the auctioneers decided that auctions were not the best way of selling laundry equipment, and moved to a private treaty approach.

The first dry-cleaning shop we had opened was in Huyton village, a fair sized shopping centre which, like Topsy, had 'just growed'. It was ripe for re-development, and word reached us around 1960 that a major developer was planning to do just that. My first reaction was to reach for our lease; to my horror it was nearly up, with only months to go. An immediate approach to the landlord secured his agreement to a new lease, and this was signed up very rapidly indeed. In due time, the developer contacted us to secure our agreement to vacate. But we had a fourteen-year lease that had almost the whole of its time to run! Negotiations began, but stalled. Meanwhile, work redeveloping continued all around. Finally, there came a point where he couldn't do any more till he got us out. We occupied a very central corner site. The payment agreed was £5,000—in today's money, certainly not less than £90,000, perhaps more. In life one needs a little bit of luck from time to time!

Meanwhile, Cleggs and Vavasseur had signed a profit sharing contract to build seventy-two flats. For this purpose we formed a new company called Lancaster Court (Chorley) Ltd., using the Chorley Laundry documentation and renaming it. The architects who had assisted in getting consent were appointed, a firm called Robinson Good based in Bolton. Chartered surveyors Johnson Kelly were selling agents, and advised on the market. Builders were chosen and a fixed price contract secured. There had been a recession (the same one that had been hurting Cleggs) and builders were very keen for business. A few months later, as a building boom got underway, we would never have secured a fixed price.

The contract called for a completion date, which if breached would activate ascertained and liquidated damages. If my memory serves, the build time was about eighteen months, but as construction boomed the builder struggled to get enough skilled people, and he began to lose momentum. In the event he was way over his contract time, and at the end we were awarded very substantial damages. Continuing my earlier practice, I kept in very close touch with Vavasseur. As time passed, house prices were rising, at first steadily, later dramatically. There came a time when anticipated profit was being recalculated upwards monthly! It was all fools gold. Heath had come into office as Prime Minister with Barber as his Chancellor. Both were determined to get the economy moving again and did so by the easy method of increasing the volume of money. Instead of going into the modernising of industry, which had been their intention, it nearly all fed into property with predictable results. Bust followed boom, and it was to prove some bust.

One morning a phone call came from the local manager of my Nat. West branch. The Area Director would very much like to meet me, and would I join him for lunch? Eating other people's food for them has never been a problem, and yes, I would be available (Richard has inherited this agreeable characteristic, and was christened by his siblings, Richard the Available!) and a date was fixed. The local manager took me to what was my first experience of bank hospitality. There are few who know how to entertain better, and there were to be a number of such occasions in the years ahead, with several different banks. One thing that became noticeable, the client was encouraged to drink very freely, but the hosts were abstemious. *In vino veritas*!'

In essence, they had been watching what the company was doing and wanted to replace Vavasseur as lender. My response was to point out that they had been approached first, but had turned us down, a fact of which they were aware. It just didn't feel right to abandon the party who had helped when others wouldn't. This was understood and perhaps respected. Before leaving though, I did make it clear that if there were ever a problem they would be my first call. On my way home one thought was, 'it was nice to be wanted'! What had been learnt was that there was a body above the local manager to turn to if need be.

As work progressed, Lavery made it very clear that funds were available for anything we had in mind, and further began to urge a second building programme to roll in the anticipated profits from Lancaster Court to minimise tax. This was the sort of offer that commercial dreams are made of, and it wasn't long before all sorts of things were in my mind!

Joe Skeaping had four children, three girls and a boy. He had set all his hopes and plans on the boy taking over from him, and indeed Keith did begin to work in his father's business. (When will parents stop trying to push their children into preconceived slots!) It just didn't work. Joe was rather highly strung, and would give the boy no freedom of action. Keith spent some time with me at Prescot where he opened his heart on how impossible it all was. A long talk with Joe resulted in a promise to try to give the boy his head, at least to some extent. Joe couldn't, in the last analysis, change his spots. Keith left to forge his own future, and Joe was deeply hurt, but recognised he had only himself to blame. From that time on he lost all interest and motivation, and asked whether we would be interested in buying his business. We were, and negotiations began. Lavery advised the cash would be available.

Almost simultaneously, word reached me that the Pioneer Laundry was on the rocks and available. Pioneer in its heyday had been the largest laundry in the North West with a payroll of some 600. Its success had been down to the M.D., one McCoombe. He had died very suddenly of a heart attack, and left a void which his wife, as chief shareholder, was quite unable to fill. That started a battle between the senior managers to be the top dog, while the interests of the business suffered. The combination of recession and inflation had finished the job. By the time we started discussions the payroll was down to about 65.

On going into a company, the first thing to be done was to install our own accounting system, and then compare the costs with Prescot. This was done immediately at Pioneer as well, and at once a huge deviation in water consumption appeared. Instructions were given to ensure that all water outlets were securely turned off at the end of the day and the readings checked next morning. There had been a very large consumption of water. Obviously, somewhere there was a substantial leak. Water people were alerted and a break in the incoming water main was soon located and repaired. It turned out to be in the main driveway, at a point just under the boardroom window. One of the Pioneer board members was a consultant who earned his keep advising laundries how to become more efficient! On checking through the figures, the leak had been in existence for several years. It hadn't caused any ground subsidence because Pioneer was built over a stream called 'Silvermere', and the leak was simply pouring straight into the stream. Pioneer had called their dry-cleaning division after this stream. Over the years thousands of pounds in excess water charges had been paid.

It had earlier become clear that Sketchley were also interested in Pioneer, so we withdrew; there was no way we could match their depth of pocket—they were a national company many times our size. Then we learnt that they had pulled out. We never did discover why, for it ultimately proved to be one of our most profitable deals. Back in the running, and with funds assured by Lavery, we concluded the purchase. Whilst in the boardroom signing up, downstairs a council official was waiting with an order to shut down the boiler, because some mechanical defects were resulting in it making excessive smoke. The company had received several warnings, but hadn't the money to do the work. Shutting the boiler meant shutting the company, so it was pointed out to the official that would mean sixty-five people being put on the dole. The fault would be dealt with in seven days—and this he accepted. It was.

From time to time I found myself puzzled that a firm such as Sketchley should not have been more active in what was effectively the rationalising of the industry. Like virtually all industries, laundries began as a mass of small, privately owned units, moving over time to bigger and fewer. Being involved brought many advantages. We were able to secure an adequate level of growth without the need for a large sales overhead cost. The sale of surplus assets invariably more than covered their cost. Most of all, though, was the huge potential in a planning consent, a potential very few seemed to be aware of—even the owners, and it wasn't my business to tell them! It was this last that made several of our deals such winners.

There was no possible future for Pioneer, but they had some valuable contracts, including the other half of Heinz and a useful amount of workwear rental. This was moved to Prescot and some domestic work to Dexter, which had by this time passed into our ownership. The Dexter was situated between Dexter Street and Upper Stanhope Street in the Toxteth area of Liverpool, and a stone's throw from the Anglican cathedral. Upper Stanhope Street was where a certain Alois Hitler had lived. He owned a restaurant in the centre of town. His home, now demolished, was about a hundred yards up the road from the laundry. The Dexter had been formed out of a terraced house whose garden had been built over, and later extended as demolition of adjacent property enabled a further extension to be built. In its day the terrace had been very upmarket. The house which became the start of the factory had as its first occupant the Harrison family, owners of a well known shipping company. A few doors further down was a house first owned by one Gladstone, father of the sometime Prime Minister!

The most senior manager at Pioneer was appointed general manager of the Dexter and took up his office immediately. Pioneer was closed, offers of employment at Dexter were accepted by a number of Pioneer people, and transport arrangements introduced to make it possible. All stores went to Prescot; though these were limited, they had been living hand to mouth. Some machinery went to Dexter, and the rest sold together with the unwanted turnover.

The company owned several houses and one or two shops, all of which were sold. The funds generated made a material impact on the borrowing, but the factory remained. It was, like Chorley, a non-conforming user and the authority again only too glad to have the prospect of getting rid of it. We were quickly granted consent for thirty-eight semi-detached houses. This time I told Lavery we had enough on our plates without taking on the development ourselves. He agreed. It was sold to a developer called Berkley Homes. Before contracts were signed, the agent advised he had received a higher offer. My response was to stay with the deal in being, but told the agent to advise our client of this offer, and tell him that in exchange for staying with him, we wanted a very rapid contract and completion. It moved like greased lightning. The money was sufficient to eliminate the borrowing on the Dexter, the Pioneer, and a small laundry we had bought in the meantime called the Widnes Ideal Laundry, and still left some money to ease the borrowing on Lancaster Court.

Lavery had been pressing for another site to roll assumed Lancaster profits into, and thus to minimise tax. An eleven acre site in Appleby, Cumbria, had been located that seemed to have good potential for second homes at rather lower cost than obtained in the National Park area. It was decided to buy it, put roads and services in and then build on, and/or sell, serviced plots. This was completed shortly before clinching the Pioneer, which was a pity. Pioneer would have made an excellent site to roll those hoped for Lancaster profits into. There is no doubt that, in retrospect, Appleby was my mistake. The timing was wrong. And this was a world where if the timing is wrong, nothing will come right. It was to prove a very costly error.

At the time the folly of Appleby, for which I bore the sole responsibility, was not apparent and all appeared to be satisfactory. The family were growing, and the need was felt for more space if each of the children were to have their own bedroom. A major house extension programme was begun. This included an indoor swimming pool with sauna, changing area and cloakroom facilities, an extension to the drawing room, and also the kitchen, plus two more bedrooms and a further bathroom. The children were excited about the pool, and made good use of it in the years ahead. It proved a perfect way to entertain their friends when there was a party. They would all disappear into the pool, and we wouldn't see them until emerging to consume, like locusts, every last scrap of food on the table!

Our next-door neighbours, Patricia and Alastair Pilkington, had a cottage in Patterdale which they were kind enough to let us use. In return they used our pool whenever they wanted. The cottage proved very popular with the children. There was a beck running through the garden and Alastair had built a canoe for use on it. One of the Pilkington children now owns it and still our children and now grandchildren make their way there. Our neighbours on the other side, once the pool was in being, gave us a sign that read 'We don't swim in your lavatory, please don't pee in our pool!' This did not meet with Judy's approval, but because they occasionally came and swam, it had to be put up. The next spring-clean all the bits and pieces had to come down for dusting, and somehow that sign never did get put back up! Their car registration number was FOO 1. It took only the smallest adaptation to make it read FOOL!

Overall at this point, Cleggs were making very satisfactory profits once again, courtesy of the various moves that had been made, and very busy with good quality work. Dexter had shaken down quickly to the new regime, and was also in good shape. Joe, as he lost interest, had cut the operation down to a three and a half day week. The work from Pioneer, overnight, brought that back to a full week. Heinz, as an American company, had a policy of never putting all its business in a given category to one supplier, and they summoned me to meet their personnel director. He explained the company policy and asked which half would we like to shed. My suggestion was that we kept it all, but split it between the two factories. This he finally agreed to, provided we kept the two company names separate! We did. In short, the laundry businesses were in good shape.

RUNNING INTO DANGER

Lancaster's build programme was losing ground steadily, and plainly going to miss its contract completion by a wide margin. This didn't appear a serious issue, for we were protected by the damages provision in the contract, and anyway the delay was simply increasing the selling price of the flats. Appleby was underway, architects appointed and the builder on site. There seemed to be no major problems. It was the calm before the storm!

In October 1973 a small news item was picked up by Joe, who after the sale of his business used to come out to Prescot every week and we would go over current events. There are inevitably a number of things in the running of a business that cannot be discussed even with senior managers. Joe was the soul of discretion. Discussion could, and did, range over any and every subject, knowing it would never go further. He was the nearest thing I ever had to a commercial 'alter ego', and something I found very valuable.

Joe had heard that a small fringe bank called 'London and Counties' had gone into receivership. Jeremy Thorpe was a major shareholder in it, at that time leader of the Liberal Party. This precipitated what was to prove one of the most dramatic collapses in property and confidence in English commercial history. All but one of a hundred fringe banks went under. Nat. West's chairman had to make a statement to the effect that the bank was not going broke, though their shares fell below par, and they therefore lost their trustee status. The government had to form a 'lifeboat' to stop major lending institutions from going bust. Those that were effectively lost were put into this 'lifeboat' and supported by the government. Dominion Trust, a very large H.P. business, was one such—there were many others. Small fry were allowed to go to the wall. Overnight, almost no lender wanted to know about property. Vavasseur was among the failures—it joined all the other fringe banks down the tubes.

Some indication of the devastating situation was a phone call from Pidgeon, the M.D. of Berkley who had bought the Pioneer site only weeks before. He asked me to buy it back. His opening pitch was a figure less than half what he had paid for it only weeks earlier. How much it could have been obtained for after haggling will never be known; we suddenly found we had massive problems of our own and couldn't have bought a hencoop at that time! On reflection it had been well to reject the higher offer, for it would not have got to contract before the storm broke.

It was not long before a phone call from Vavasseur's London office came through, though not Lavery—he had been summarily dismissed. "We want our money back," was the stark message, "and we want it now." At this stage, though, useful sums had been repaid from the various gains on the laundry side; the company still owed not much less than a million. In today's money a multiple of twelve or possibly more would obtain. This was secured on Lancaster and Appleby, but—and this was to prove onerous—with cross guarantees on Cleggs. My first move was a call to the area director of Nat. West. We had a good lunch, but did not find it possible to enjoy it as in former times! He was sympathetic, but effectively said, "Sorry, but we have our own problems."

Within a day or two of that meeting with Nat. West, there was a call from Johnson Kelly; they had a party interested in buying the whole Chorley development. Central Lancashire New Town was a new authority, charged with developing the area, but were finding a real bar to industry coming into the district was an acute shortage of executive standard housing. They had examined the flats, now at last virtually complete, and were impressed. In their day, and in that part of the world, they set a new standard for that type of accommodation. They saw them as the answer to their need. I got in touch with Vavasseur, who had earlier said to forget about profit share—just give them their money back and ask them to confirm this in writing. They did.

The next move was to arrange with Nat. West's merchant banking arm to repay the amount to be received from the purchaser, over £700k, to Vavasseur. This they did, but not before the deal was solid and they were not exposed in any way. Concurrently, I had indicated to Vavasseur that they could expect around £750k very shortly, but that the remaining exactly £200k would have to wait for some time, though we would, of course, pay interest on the outstanding balance. They could hardly believe their ears, and assured me there was no problem about the balance—anytime would do, just get them the larger amount back. My failure to get this as a binding commitment before releasing the cash was a serious oversight. Certainly it was a time of some strain, and there were moments of considerable tiredness. It might also have owed something to the trust and friendly relations that had been built in earlier times. Whatever the reason, I failed to do it, and it was to prove a serious lapse.

Within a week of getting the money, they were back demanding the rest, a demand that couldn't be met then or in the foreseeable future, other than through profits from the laundry side. A writ was issued and battle commenced. Because the matter was of vital interest to the company's future, we retained a senior barrister and a junior, for if we lost it would spell the end of the business. They were optimistic, had already had dealings with other Vavasseur clients and said, "This time we will give them a bloody nose!" They seemed confident that the profit sharing agreement would prevail over the banking relationship. They were clear that Vavasseur's abandonment of the profit share arrangement was irrelevant, and were proved right on that point.

The case was set down for hearing in the High Court of Chancery and took two days. At the suggestion of the senior barrister, I spent some considerable time preparing an analysis, and in some detail, of the whole affair, right from the beginning, having carefully indexed and summarised it. In the event he spent most of his time quoting from it. I could have done the job better myself, if only because of my greater familiarity with the issues. That said, I'm aware that the man who is his own lawyer has a fool for a client!

If the affair had not been so serious it would have been hilarious. We four, my solicitor sitting on my right, the junior immediately behind him, and the senior to the juniors immediately to the left, were a compact little group. There were a number of occasions as the case proceeded when I wanted to make a point. The obvious thing was to turn round and alert the senior, who was after all, just behind me. No, no, that wouldn't do at all! It must needs be written down and passed to my solicitor, who read it and passed it behind to the junior, who read it, and who then passed it to the senior, who read it. And who may, or may not, as the case may be, do something about it! The performance was conducted in reverse if the senior wanted to raise a matter with me!

By the end of the first day my team were clearly worried; they had picked up the drift of the judge's mind, one Mr Justice Templeman, and didn't like it. They suggested an attempt to compromise with the plaintiff. My response was that they had been confident we would win, and we would therefore continue. We desperately needed to win. The outcome was that the judge found for Vavasseur on the grounds that the banking covenant took precedence over the commercial profit sharing arrangement.

Asked if we wanted to appeal, the answer was, "Yes, very definitely." If nothing else it bought a little time, or so I thought. Leaving the court, my solicitor, the same Jim Wotherspoon (we had been pals from school days) turned to me and said, "Morris, you are finished."

I replied: "No, we have a fortnight's stay whilst the appeal is heard. I can use that time."

Jim's response was: "The stay is only on Lancaster Court; you have cross guarantees on Cleggs. They will want a receiver in the laundry side tomorrow."

My next question: "Do you have to agree?"

"No, but they will go straight to court for an order."

"How long will that take them?"

"Two days," he replied. "At the very outside three, but more likely two."

My mind has seldom been as concentrated as at that moment. From the courthouse corridor the Area Director of Nat. West was rung, and I asked for a meeting with the Regional Director the following morning. I already knew the amount needed was outside the Area Director's discretion, and even if he wanted to, he wouldn't be able to move fast enough. This was agreed—the Area Director came with me to the Regional Head office in King Street, Manchester. John Burgess was the man and I took to him at once. Burgess had already been briefed, but nonetheless, I went through my argument, pointing out we had only turned to Vavasseur after being refused by Nat. West and that a sense of loyalty kept me with them when Nat. West changed their minds. Also that the bank had said to come back to them if a problem arose; also, that we had banked with them throughout the life of the company. Finally, that all their capital would be repaid and every penny of interest met in full and on schedule. At the conclusion of my case, Burgess didn't speak to me, but turned to his subordinate and said, "Get a firm grip on everything he has got, and wire the money to Vavasseur today." That moment is burnt in my memory and will never be forgotten. It meant we lived to fight another day.

When the debt was cleared, I wrote to John to thank him for his confidence, and we had a gala dinner at View Road for the three levels of bank manager—local, area, and regional, and their wives. It has passed through my mind on odd occasions that had John been ill or on holiday, that would have been the end of Cleggs, for it was not likely that any other party in the bank would have had the authority, or the will, to make a favourable decision at a time when the bank was itself struggling. On meeting John that first time there was an instant chemistry beyond my power to explain, but which translated into my confidence in him and his trust in me. Jimmy had been right in his forecast. Vavasseur's lawyers were on the phone next morning asking our agreement to the appointment of receivers. As instructed, he refused, and before they could get an order the matter was resolved.

After we had moved to Gawsworth, Alastair Pilkington and his wife came to stay with us for a couple of days. Alastair had been our next-door neighbour in Rainhill for over twenty years. An engineer by profession, he was the inventor of the world beating float glass process for making flat glass, and in doing so had really put Pilkingtons on the map. It was this that gained him his knighthood and in due course he became chairman. I knew that the company banked with Nat. West. It was the reason that the St. Helens branch was the largest outside London. So when deciding whom to invite for a dinner party, it occurred to me that Alastair must know John Burgess. John and his wife, who now lived at Prestbury only a couple of miles down the road, joined us for that occasion and it was a happy gathering.

The saga is not quite ended. Because an order had been made against the company by the court, the court had to rescind it on Vavasseur receiving satisfaction. So an appearance in court was required. My solicitor and I duly appeared before the same Mr Justice Templeman. On the situation being explained to him, he said, "Ah, yes, now that is the nice young man [I was in my early forties, but Templeman was much older!) with the well presented case—application granted." Such a kindly disposition would have been more welcome had it been in evidence a little earlier! That was to prove the tightest corner of my commercial life; it would probably be quite hard to get closer to the edge without actually falling over!

On arriving home after losing the case, there had been no option but to share the position with Judy. The family had always been Judy's chief interest and concern—commercial matters never aroused her enthusiasm. In the day-to-day ups and downs of the business she had no interest. This, however, was in a different category altogether. Our home would be forfeit; everything had always been ploughed back into the company, so there were no personally held reserves to fall back on. I wasn't even eligible for unemployment benefit, being self-employed! (After that I made myself an employee of the company!)

The future was unknown and likely to be bleak. The thing that hurt the most was that the children would have to leave their schools and continue in the state sector. If one is considering private education, it is almost certainly better never to start than to have to finish midway. My mother had only what she received from the company and it would have been unrealistic to expect any help from Banny, who was sending his own children to grant aided day schools. Judy was philosophical and totally supportive. Before that meeting next morning with the bank, there was one very long night, but sheer exhaustion sent me into a dreamless sleep. None of these problems had been shared with the children; they had their own studies to pursue. If the worst happened, there would be time to explain before the end of term—fees had been paid up until then. One last 'nasty' before the affair was ended—we had to pay not only our own legal fees, but those of the plaintiff as well. Between the two, this amounted to about £15,000—a large figure at that time.

As noted earlier, the events of the past couple of years had put the laundry side into excellent shape; both factories were performing well and producing good profits. The servicing and reducing of the £200k loan was fairly heavy, but within our capacity. With only Appleby as an ongoing development, my time was devoted very largely to the laundry side. Whilst purchasing more laundries was, at least for a time, out of the question, we were still able to buy turnover whenever the right sort became available, which it did from time to time. This was a useful supplement to our own sales efforts.

There were other helpful developments. Government had become very alarmed at increasing unemployment, and was introducing all manner of grants and subsidies to try and stem the rising tide. My own view was that they merely distorted management decisions, and such as de-rating industry would have been far more efficient. Nonetheless, if government was making grants available, my job was to ensure we got our fullest share. It was around this time that there was a remarkable transformation in the Labour government's approach to private enterprise. Almost, one went to bed one night a grinder of the faces of the poor, and woke up the next morning a valued provider of jobs!

Something called 'work experience' was introduced whereby industry employed youngsters who couldn't get work for up to a year at government expense. Until the scheme was abolished, we had half a dozen or more at each plant providing very useful savings on our payroll. One side effect was that, in some sense, these youngsters were on an extended interview, and we were able to offer proper jobs to the best when their work experience time was up—a useful contribution to raising the quality of the people we employed. Grants for capital equipment were also on offer and secured.

On one occasion an official came to my office to finalise an application. When it was done he asked whether there were any other claim we would like to have considered! Vehicles had been excluded, but an amendment that had escaped me brought commercials within the scope of grant aid. He mentioned this, and, yes, we had bought a couple of vans within the last year. "Those," he said delightedly, "qualify"—and out came more application forms. This was during Harold Wilson's last administration, later to be led by Jim Callaghan. It was always easier to get money out of a Labour than a Tory government. With the advent of Mrs Thatcher, a very chill wind quickly began to blow down the grant corridors. But by this time I had become, and remained, really quite an expert at getting everything that was properly and lawfully available!

In the two years it took to clear the bank loan, we were still able to make progress in several areas. Next door to us, and fronting onto the main road, the Parish Rooms came onto the market. This was a solidly built turn of the century structure—a natural for us to secure, even though we had no immediate use for it. The deal was done, so we had some reserve space for the future. Internally was also a fruitful time. By this time domestic work had completely finished at Prescot, though some still continued at Dexter. The domestic dry-cleaning shops had all been closed; the only dry-cleaning now being done was commercial. The frontage at Prescot had been turned into a 'coin op'. This last was quite successful for a few years, until we needed the space for the then expanding garment rental.

BACK ON AN EVEN KEEL

Still the question of motivating our people nagged away at me. Payroll remained the largest single cost, and its control therefore fundamental to success. It followed that if this could be kept at a given level, the company would be profitable. Working back from the bottom line, and using the previous three years as a guide, a 'target percentage' was arrived at. We then discussed the idea with our people, and secured general agreement after some resistance, not least from management. If the payroll exceeded the target, only the basic rate would be paid; if it didn't, the gap between the target and the actual would be put into a separate account, irrespective of how much it was, and the money paid out twice a year in the early summer and Christmas. This account was controlled by two signatories from the factory floor. Because the two categories of work going through the plant required very different labour input, a correction factor was worked out to adjust the target percentage accordingly.

The scheme worked well from day one, and produced some interesting fall out. It might be asked why we didn't embrace a straightforward profit sharing scheme based on audited profits? The reason was that there are many factors that affect profits for better or worse, but over which both the blue and white collars had no influence. Even if profit was taken just at the operating level, there were still significant variables that were beyond their control. By linking incentive payments to payroll ensured that this was an area over which they had very material sway, for they were the payroll.

Time was also a factor. I had sufficient confidence in our internal figures to work from those. This meant that at the end of each month a figure of the amount to be transferred could be published. This allowed the fiscally literate to easily work out how much was accruing per capita on an ongoing basis. This played an important role in maintaining interest. Working from audited profits would have meant a long delay and no interim or ongoing information.

We had never had a sickness payment scheme. I refused absolutely to have the standard type common in industry, where everyone could be off sick for a given number of weeks and receive full pay. There was far too much abuse of these schemes, and I was outraged when hearing people say "I've had my holidays but haven't taken my sick leave yet"! Once our target payroll scheme was underway we devised our own. This divided the company into sections, each electing two members to form a 'sickness committee', a member of management making the third. If someone from their section was off, they would meet to decide whether the absence was genuine. If it was, they would be paid, otherwise not. The management member only voted if there was a tie between the elected members. If the vote was unfavourable to the party, they could appeal to the full works committee whose decision was final. The underlying principal was one of the oldest in English jurisprudence—trial by jury!

Explaining it to everyone, the response was somewhat sceptical, but given it represented an advance on what had gone before, it was accepted. The sickness committees duly elected, and the thing launched, it worked like a dream. The elected folk took their duties seriously and if someone, claiming to be off with a bad back, was known to have been out dancing, there was no way they were going to be paid, doctor's note or no doctor's note. They were far tougher than management could possibly have been. In a small town people know what other people are doing, and word invariably got round if the party was swinging the lead, or shopping, or whatever. It was also not lost on them that payments were a charge on the target percentage. In this way the sickness scheme and the payroll target interlocked.

An unexpected gain from our bespoke scheme was that the genuinely ill could expect to be paid, not for some arbitrary period like a month, but indefinitely.

There were at least one or two cases where payment was made for several months—a result that was only possible because virtually all specious claims were being disallowed. The money was going to the genuinely ill, not being dissipated on fraudulent claims. There were very few appeals to the works committee, reflecting the fact that the sickness committees were well informed and making accurate assessments. In description it may sound rather cumbersome; in practice very little time was taken up in its application. There also developed a lively interest in the elections that were held bi-annually, aided perhaps by the sense that it was a role that had a genuine purpose.

Another way the target percentage worked was on getting a large new order. Management would advise the works committee that it would support, say, two extra employees whilst still contributing to the target percentage. On occasions they would discuss it among themselves, and decide to try and manage with one extra person. They were well aware that the whole of the pay for that one missing person would go straight into the kitty. The bottom line for measuring its success was that our absenteeism due to sickness was comfortably below 2%. When it is noted that there are groups where absence touches 10%, and occasionally (coal mining) even more, we might have a measure of just how much lead swinging goes on.

Over the years the enthusiasm of the workforce for union membership had dwindled. Then a call from Heinz came through to say that they had just agreed a closed shop arrangement with their unions. This meant our transport would not be allowed to enter their premises unless the drivers held a union card. Heinz was too good an order to lose. The drivers had to be asked to join a union of their choice and the company would pay the subscriptions. They chose, not surprisingly, the T. & G., at that time one of the strongest, and sometimes most aggressive, unions. This reawakened interest in union membership generally on the factory floor, and a fair number of our people signed up.

Before long the District Official, one Ron White, called to make himself known, a very large man with a bushy beard. We got on all right; from my side there were a few non-negotiables. No closed shop. No objection to 100% membership if that's what 100% of our folk wanted, but no compulsion. Nor would I agree to communicate with our people through the union. This was accepted. Ron on his side said he would never come to the factory to talk to his members without first coming to see me. For my part it didn't really matter whether he did or didn't. Unions do tend to be very correct in these sorts of ways.

There came a time when the union movement, in their dispute with government, discovered that they could bring the entire N.H.S. to a standstill by the simple expedient of calling out the hospital laundry workers. N.H.S. carried about 48hr. stocks of linen. They started to use this weapon. Hospitals turned to the private sector for help. Few responded, fearing union wrath. But we were a union place. Getting our people together they were asked if they were willing to have a go, indicating it would have a very significant effect on the target percentage, since we would be charging full list price for everything. Both we and the hospitals knew that there was no question of a longer term relationship; they did, after all, have their own 'in house' laundries. They said 'yes'. We set up an evening shift, and the stuff poured in. At the end of the first week the figures posted on the board showed bonuses of as much as the basic rate. Pay had doubled overnight!

After a couple of weeks the union had got wind, and along came Ron: "We can't 'ave this, its strike breaking." Knowing he would not yet have spoken to his shop stewards, my suggestion was that he have a chat with them, and then we could have a cup of coffee and discuss the problem. I learnt later that he was almost manhandled out of the building by his members, and he never did get that cup of coffee. We did work for the hospitals on each occasion their laundries were called out. And each time our people were far and away the highest paid operatives in the industry! Our labours ensured that some beds were kept open for the most urgent cases. It isn't every day that substantial monetary gain can be combined with the moral high ground! After a while the unions realised they were getting so much negative publicity that they jacked it in.

My sister had pursued a varied career, ranging from hotel management, to teaching, to working with the United Nations Association. This last she did for a number of years, working on projects in Greece and Egypt. Sometimes when on furlough she would spend a few weeks with us, perhaps working in a shop or some such. The work with the U.N.A. was very worthwhile, but attracted hardly any pay, so she needed to top up her funds from time to time. Gradually the attractions of travel faded, and she came to work with us full time. She became involved in production, and proved to be a natural as a production manager. She kept right on top of her staff and little in the way of evasive action got past her. Indeed, almost the only time the union official Ron got involved was when she had been pretty tough, and the girls had complained to him. In he would come, complete with beard, and he would open up:

"They won't 'ave it, you know!"

"What won't they have, Ron?"

"Your sister driving them like that."

Thus the conversation got going, and it was possible to point out that not all his members were angels, perfect in all their ways. We pointed out, furthermore, that we were working to very tight schedules, and if they were not maintained, he would very shortly have no members here. It would invariably end up that he would explain to his stewards that management had commercial imperatives to deal with that wouldn't go away, and for my part I would have a quiet word with my sister. My side of the bargain was always carried out; I'm not so sure he did his! However, things never reached crisis level, and we had open lines of communication within the factory.

The question of maintaining schedule was critically important. Some of our clients imposed very stringent conditions. Ford, for example, required their work to be collected during a twenty minute 'window' in the morning. Miss the window and they put the driver through hoops, the better to encourage him not to miss again! The work had to he returned the same afternoon, again to a timed window. Food processors, large users of laundry services, seldom had more than forty-eight hour stocks of clean linen, some only twenty-four hours. When we first secured Heinz they pointed out that forty-eight hours after we stopped, they would have to shut down. The thought of being responsible for closing down a factory employing a couple of thousand workers didn't bear thinking about. We made sure everyone in the company knew about schedule!

In the later seventies Dexter was beginning to struggle. The general manager was a good chap, but not perhaps strong enough. The mix of work was not helpful, with domestic still being processed there, and not enough commercial to outweigh it. We had processed washed jeans for a period, but they attracted burglars like filings to a magnet. Insurers began to demand we turn the place into a Fort Knox, so that ended that line. There were only a very few privately owned laundries left on Greater Merseyside by this time, and of those none were shutting just then. The decision was taken to close, transfer all the contract work to Prescot, and dispose of the domestic. Jobs at Prescot were offered and some accepted. But, as with other closures, the lure of a lump sum of cash in hand, in the shape of redundancy payments, was irresistible for many. Transport arrangements were made to bring those who stayed with us, and take them home again at the end of the day. The buildings found a ready market and were quickly sold. Prescot was now bulging at the seams and consideration was given to bringing the Parish Rooms into use. The problem here was a vehicular alleyway that separated the two properties and would have made the logistics far from ideal. It was decided to soldier on as long as possible with the one place, aided by putting on a permanent evening shift.

In 1978 word was about that the National Coal Board were planning to put all their miners into a workwear rental scheme. Coal had long been one of the largest employers. In the early part of the century some 750,000 men toiled in the mines. Slowly over the years with the growth of alternative fuels and mechanisation, this had fallen to about 250,000. That was still very much business to be reckoned with. Every firm in the country with an established workwear rental business was invited to show interest. We did, and on day one! To our astonishment, we discovered that hardly any companies, including some of the large nationals, were interested. The reason, it emerged, was that a certain Mr Scargill was just coming into office as the President of the National Union of Mineworkers. He was replacing the steady, middle of the road, Joe Gormley. Scargill had earned a reputation for extreme militancy. As head of the strongest union in the country there was much apprehension about his moves, and the feeling in our industry was to keep one's distance. Workwear always involved any union that was represented at the client—it was their members who were going to wear it! The one thing safer than using a long spoon to sup with the devil was not to sup with him at all! In the event, and over the next few years, he met his match in

Mrs Thatcher, being utterly defeated and destroying his union in the process—a union that was known as the Praetorian Guard of the movement.

But we were a union place, and having long learned to live with them, none of these fears weighed in our reckoning. N.C.B. officials came out to inspect the place, and we showed them the Parish Rooms that would be fitted out and dedicated to their work if we won a slice of it. That helped, and after some of the easiest negotiations, we were awarded about thirteen thousand wearers. The price agreed was about 80p per wearer, per week. We would have been happy to take the business at 2Op less. Undermining their negotiating team was the fact they were having difficulty in getting enough interest to cover the whole country. We would have taken more, but were at the limit of our financial strength. Good profits were being made, and we hadn't spent the cash from the sale of the Dexter buildings. Also, our relations with Nat. West were quite excellent; they had seen their £200k emergency loan dealt with as promised, and we had never defaulted by a day or a penny on any of their money. The local manager also knew that recourse to John Burgess could be had if need be. The cost of the garments, which included underwear and socks as well as the top gear, was half a million pounds. To this was added the expenditures to get the Parish Rooms ready and fitted out with the necessary machinery. Steam and air were brought across the alley from our existing services. The bank gave all the help that was needed.

The contract was for three years, though in fact it overran by almost a year, a hugely beneficial extension from our point of view. In addition, the level of absenteeism at the mines was extraordinarily high; we seldom got more than 75% of the numbers a mine was entitled to send. But they were paying for 100%. If they went on strike, not an unknown phenomenon in the mining world, we still got paid, though a couple of years into the contract an official in the N.C.B. suggested they ought to have a rebate, to which we agreed. If they didn't use the service when on holiday, we still got paid. And the N.C.B. couldn't go bust! It was a contract made in heaven!

Except Mr Scargill. We knew that from time to time miners would visit. We had long made a practice of entertaining key people among our good customers. It seemed wise, therefore, to get a few facts. It emerged that the government subsidy to the N.C.B. equalled the cost of their entire payroll! At the next works committee these facts were spelt out; also that government has no money of its own—only what it takes from you and me. This meant therefore that our people were paying taxes that contributed to the funding of the very high rates of pay enjoyed by the miners. All of this registered. When the visits began and as, inevitably, they talked about wages, they wanted to know what our people earned. On learning the amount, the response was, "We wouldn't get out of bed for that!" In those days miners were the aristocrats of the working world. Our folk were ready, and it came back to me that they had given better than they got. "Try earning your own money instead of taking it from us taxpayers, and we would have more in our packets" was the sort of answer they gave. No manager could have said that, but *they* could, and did. From that quarter it was accepted. Like calls unto like.

It goes without saying that this contract made a very useful contribution to a reduction in payroll percentage and therefore a very large boost to the amount going into bonus. There were times when we got our production payroll usefully below 20%. The bottom line for the company was a massive jump in profitability; bank borrowing evaporated, and there was a serious danger that we could start to pay substantial corporation tax.

Now corporation tax was, in my understanding, largely a voluntary tax, and we had not been in the habit of volunteering! We were situated in what was defined as a 'Special Development Area'. This meant we could write off all capital expenditure, except buildings, in the year of purchase. In the case of new buildings, initial and annual allowance added up to about 10% in the first year. Provided capital purchases were equal to profits, no tax would be payable. For many, if not most years, therefore, only relatively modest amounts of tax were due. In exchange we had very up to date plant. The coal contract changed that. There was no way we could spend our new level of profit all on machines.

When finally the contract with the N.C.B. came up for renewal, there was much greater interest. Those who had stood back first time round had noted that we hadn't had a rough time with the coal unions, and that substantial profits had been enjoyed. With a fine sense of loyalty to those who had taken the initial risk, the N.C.B. ensured that the great majority of the work stayed with them. Of all the original suppliers, we were the only company that secured an increase in the number of mines. Given that no new mines had been opened, had to mean we took some off an existing contractor. It proved to be Initial, the biggest operator in the game. The contract with the N.C.B. had provided for such a possibility and spelt out exactly how the transfer was to be made, so Initial had to follow the drill. The managers detailed to make the changeover did so with absolute loathing—they hated us for it. It was perhaps a David and Goliath type situation!

Operating in two separate buildings was not ideal, and the volume of work going through was such that efficiency was being lost through overcrowding. The decision was taken to find a greenfield site and put up a purpose built factory. A site of about four acres was quickly identified, but planning consent was very slow in coming—ultimately over a year. This gave plenty of time to apply for the grants that were available in S.D.A's, but Maggie had come to power and her handbag was closed! It took months of very vigorous debate to secure what the legislation provided for. It reached a point where, in my arguments with the quite senior official whose task it was to not pay any grants, that I took a dictionary with me to support my definition of the meaning of words! In the event we became almost good friends! Because of the delays in getting consent it was further possible to argue that we wouldn't proceed unless the government honoured its clearly stated provisions. They finally did, and the grant was worth about £100k.

There was a fierce recession in 1980. Labour had let rip the public purse before the 1979 election to try and help their electoral chances. The Tories won, and Geoffrey Howe, the Chancellor, had put the brakes on heavily. Commercial building almost ground to a halt, and there was a huge rise in bankruptcies. Builders were desperate for work. It was at this point we came into the market for a 50,000 sq.ft. new build. We were able to get an outstandingly good fixed price contract, and a very high build specification. My architect had produced a splendid external appearance; my concern was with the interior, for everything learnt during the last thirty plus years was built into the place. When a new structure is on the cards it is easy to do things that might be virtually impossible to add later, such as collecting water off the roof. Heat recovery systems were built into the floor of the wash house, offices were heated with condensate from the machines, and many other innovations. It was an exciting time.

There was one sobering moment when, one evening after work, I walked down to the building site to see how things had gone during the day. A man exercising his dog stopped alongside me, paused, drew on his pipe and said, "You might well look—factories are closing all over England, and here is some stupid b—building a new one!" Having thus delivered himself, he pulled again on his pipe, called his dog to heel, and went his way. There seemed, at that moment, no special need to identify myself as the ill advised party. I walked home a little more reflectively that evening!

Once word got about that we were interested in alternative premises, half a dozen local authorities and others inundated us with lists of factories they had available with vacant possession. It had become my fixed resolve, however, to start from scratch, and produce a building that I could be proud of, but more, which was as efficient in its function as it was possible to make it. The last purpose-built laundry was before the Second World War. It had the side effect, which wasn't lost on my people, that if we sold or were taken over, whoever it was, would be highly unlikely to close it, making their jobs as secure as they ever can be in the commercial world.

Because the N.C.B. was our biggest customer, the question of coal firing raised its head. Plant was now available that was fully automated; a piece of coal was never actually seen! It was delivered in totally enclosed coal tankers and pumped into our storage silo. From there, partly by mechanical means and partly by compressed air, the coal was fed into the boiler. More to the point, grant was available from the Coal Board for the installation of coal fired equipment, and on checking consumptions it was a matter of some surprise that we would save about £35k on fuel compared with the oil we were using. This was almost exactly the amount by which our rates increased! We made sure the officials at the Doncaster offices knew we were planning to convert to coal. That got us a couple of brownie points. So, to coal we returned.

Paul, our senior engineer, had been responsible for installing all the pipework and machines in the Parish Rooms and had done a good job. When the question of fitting out the new place arose, he said he was happy to be responsible and oversee it. A special payment was agreed for this material extra task, and a plan of the positioning of all the equipment which had been worked out, given to him. This last had involved asking everyone who had an idea, to forward it for consideration, and some useful thoughts emerged. He went away happy and with some months to prepare for the job. He enjoyed my full confidence in him based on previous experience, and I left him to do his thing, having much else on my plate. From time to time I would check with him that all was going well, to be met with assurances. Then one evening at home a call came through from his wife. Paul was in a terrible state but wouldn't say what the problem was, only that it had to do with the job. Next morning, having called him to my office, he broke down and said he couldn't do the work on the new building. There was nothing for it—I told him to forget all about it and to just concentrate on his regular duties.

After he had gone, I found myself wondering where to go from there. Work on installing pipework was due to begin in as little as a month. The builders were right on schedule and any delays we imposed would incur cost. The next day a machine manufacturing sales rep. who had supplied machinery to us for many years called to see if we needed anything. Telling him of the problem, he said he thought he knew just the man—Walter Coultous, a recently retired director of a Birmingham laundry who had, a couple of years previously, been responsible for re-installing the pipework and services of a building gutted by fire. A quick phone call and he arranged for Walter Coultous to come and see me the following day.

We agreed terms and Walter accepted the job to start the next day. Having explained this development to Paul, I asked Walter to keep Paul informed of what he was doing, but not to involve him in any decisions or other input. I advised Paul to this effect, and my senior engineer was a man restored, though he never had the same confidence in himself in the future. For Paul it had been a project too far. Walter was tailor-made for the job. He set to work purposefully and had everything organised to begin installation of the various services as soon as the building was able to take them. I rather suspect he thoroughly enjoyed his job.

Because many of our clients spent substantial sums with us, and did so every week, maintaining good relations was a high priority. This included entertaining, and we were spending quite large amounts on it. It was a golden rule that either you do it properly, or leave it alone. To offer hospitality, and deliver it meanly and narrowly, is counter productive. Few things communicate so clearly to a client your assessment of him. So it was decided to create a visitor's suite in the new building. This consisted of a lounge, dining room and cloakroom with, of course, kitchen facilities. The whole was fitted out to a high standard and an *a la carte* menu produced. The client was shown into the suite where he selected his meal; then, if he hadn't been previously, he would be shown round the factory before returning to the suite for a pre-prandial and lunch. It was hugely successful; apparently one of the things that impressed most was that the client had the exclusive use of the suite, whereas in a restaurant everything was shared. Prospective clients were given similar treatment, following which we seldom failed to gain the business. The senior sales manager was usually the host; for my own part commercial entertaining consumed too much time, but I would attend if that was the sales advice.

When not being used for clients, and subject to pressure of work, on a Friday seven of the employees were invited to have an extended lunch in the suite, having chosen their meal from the menu. Everything was done to the same standard as for clients except for wine. Work had to be done in the afternoon! The manager of their section acted as host. Over a period everyone had a turn, and it proved popular. Those whose turn it was rose to the occasion, and made a special effort to dress and look their best. It was one more contribution to breaking down the 'us' and 'them' syndrome. A further move in that direction was not to have separate cloakroom facilities for management and operatives. A high standard of fittings and finishes was installed, and management's use of them helped to maintain that standard.

The move to the new building was almost a military operation, phased over three weekends. It was just not practicable to do the whole lot in one go. It meant that for a fortnight there had to be liaison between the two places as some work was being processed in both—tiresome, but manageable for a short period. The crane people were vital to a smoothly effected changeover and they served us well. Of the largest pieces, there were several of which we had only one. Had there been an accident with any one of those we should have had a major problem. In the event there wasn't.

The only major hiccup was the new boiler which was scheduled to arrive about ten days before the move, in order to give plenty of time to install, test it, and for our people to get used to its handling. No boiler and nothing happens in a laundry. Literally twenty-four hours before it was due, the makers rang to say there would be a delay of two to three weeks. Nothing would shift them. The move had to go ahead, cranes, heavy transport, engineers, everything was booked and cast in concrete. In the event we had to search for and hire two mobile boilers, and connect them up temporarily to the steam line. That apart, the whole business ran like clockwork, and by the end of the third weekend everything was up and running in the new building.

Once all was installed our own engineers were kept busy for several weeks getting the equipment to run reliably. Moving it had disturbed sensitive gear, and sediment in pipes had been loosened and kept causing blockages. In time it all settled down. The fact that in those early weeks Paul was kept very busy probably helped him to reintegrate himself and regain his self-respect.

Once underway, we had the most cost effective unit in the U.K. It was the first purpose built laundry on a greenfield site since the second world war. The plant was designed to take work in at one end, process it through the building, and load the finished orders at the other. The factory and van floor levels were the same height, which meant we could move to a roll on, roll off system. The heat recovery installations made a useful contribution to fuel economy, and we collected many tens of thousands of gallons of water from the roof in the course of a year. This had the additional advantage that not only was it free, but sewage charges were based on the metered intake of clean water! All we had to do was pass the rainwater through a sand filter, which had been built in, to make it immediately useable.

We had sought permission to sink a well, for we knew there was water not too far down—but the water authority refused. On a recent visit to the plant, they were able to say that they now had their well. The all up cost, including moving expenses, was something over a million. Given the quality of the build, it was an exceptional investment, and once the recession began to ease it would have cost very substantially more per square foot.

Another of our golden rules was, 'if there is money to be spent, let's try and keep it in the family.' Rates of pay in the industry have never been other than at the lower end. In a competitive world it is hard to dent this iron rule, and virtually impossible to defeat it. It is the simple reason why more and more straightforward, repetitive work is being located overseas, where rates of pay are a fraction of those that obtain here. But the new building gave increased opportunity to use the golden rule. There were landscaped gardens of reasonable extent to be maintained, and two of our chaps undertook this. Even at overtime rates it was less costly than putting the work to contract, and boosted the earnings of those concerned very usefully. Additionally, they took a certain pride in what they were doing—they did, after all, work there. Similarly with window cleaning and other routine jobs.

Over the previous thirty or so years we had had three fires in the old building, two of which were quite large. The pressure on everyone, particularly management, was intense on these occasions. We would inform all our clients at once. One response may be taken to typify most. The chap at the other end said, "I'm very sorry for you, but the work will be returned on schedule, won't it?!" After the third one, sprinklers were fitted, and were so as a matter of course in the new building. The reduction in insurance premiums paid for them in about four years. They are the only system yet devised that begins to put the fire out almost as soon as it begins, and without the intervention of a human being, that last being the key factor.

There is nothing like a fire to reveal a lot about the company's customers. There were those who genuinely felt sorry and said they wouldn't bother us with a claim, that we had enough to do. We were insured properly, however, and did insist on a fair claim being made in the interests of longer-term goodwill. A claims office was set up, well manned, and dealt quickly and honestly with all genuine losses. Then there were the others. One party suffered fire damage to a pair of rather average curtains. The claim arrived for a much better than average pair, together with a demand for the replacement of settee, chair, cushion covers and carpet—this on the grounds they were all matching! Similarly, a damaged dress led to a claim for shoes, gloves, and handbag as well, on more or less the same grounds! Life as a loss adjustor must have a fascinating human side to it.

The Tories had come to power in 1979, prior to which the previous Labour government had let fiscal rectitude fly out of the window in an attempt to buy voter support. A first response of the new Chancellor of the Exchequer, Mr

Howe, was to put the blocks on through a very tough budget. There were no plusses for the average citizen and several minuses. By common consent, it was a wretched budget from the consumer's point of view. However, one small clause made it, for us, simply the best budget ever. To try and stimulate commercial building, Mr Howe increased initial allowances on new commercial buildings in Special Development Areas to 100%. This was a dramatic increase from the earlier 10% that we had built into our calculations. We were in an S.D.A. and were putting up a brand new commercial building, one reason for which was to minimise corporation tax! Overnight our tax bill evaporated, and we were able to claim from the revenue many tens of thousands of pounds. It is an ill wind that blows nobody any good.

It was decided that we would have an official opening, and make a bit of a song and dance about it. Given that my attitude to unions had produced very appreciable rewards, I sounded out the T. & G. to see whether they thought Len Murray, at that time General Secretary of the T.U.C., might do the honours. He agreed. Essentially a likeable and rather shy man, we got on well. With him came some of the top brass of the T. & G., together with Ron White. We had lunch at my home, followed by the couple of minutes journey to the factory where Len moved about freely, meeting and talking with our people. His manner was easy and completely unaffected. After the ceremony there were refreshments in the visitor's suite. The shop stewards, and as many of the long serving employees as could be accommodated, were included.

It was a happy occasion, but didn't do me much good with my peers in the industry. Fraternising with the enemy, if not treason! Though advised, the trade press managed not to report what was, after all, the official opening of the first brand new build laundry for the better part of half a century. Some years after I had finished, I learnt that the plaque marking the occasion had been taken down! That's life! Fixed ideas aren't easily moved. Len in due time got a peerage, indicative perhaps of the status and power of the union movement at that time.

I was by no means unaware of the downside of the union movement, which ever since the end of the Second World War had been gaining in influence until it was too strong and aggressive for its own good. "All power corrupts"—a truism that applied to unions just as much as other power centres. My willingness to work with, and be positive towards, the unions we were involved with was, in part idealistic and more substantially, pragmatic. Idealistic, because I had read my history books. (Had anyone treated me the way 19th Century employers routinely dealt with their employees, had there not been a union, I would have formed one!) Pragmatic, because we were based in what was probably the most intensely unionised part of the U.K. As such they were a fact of life, and those who run businesses do well to accept facts. Besides which, I do believe very firmly in the right of people to associate freely. That that right was sometimes abused is a part of the price of democracy.

Once the dust had settled and I was free to give my attention to where we should next be heading, it all gave me pause for thought. There were very few privately owned laundries left in the Merseyside area, many of which we had bought. So we began to look to Manchester. The Manchester Co-op Laundry had just closed, and we were able to buy their turnover, though this approach to developing the business was clearly going to he a reducing one.

The more I thought about our future direction, the more it became clear that we had reached a watershed. Whilst now the largest privately owned workwear rental/laundry business in the North West, and able to cover that area as efficiently as any, and better than most, there was a very large part of the country where we were not represented.

Our chief competition was now the large, national and publicly quoted companies, and they could offer formidable opposition. Whilst in our new premises we could operate more efficiently than any plant in the U.K., there was nothing to stop one of the large national firms targeting our clients in terms of price. Also, there was a developing move by large clients to central buying because it tended to give them economies of scale. It was a move that placed us at a considerable disadvantage against the nationals. They had perhaps a dozen plants all over the U.K., whereas we had only the one. Asked to quote by a potential customer who had a business in Cornwall and another in the Highlands, and we would be at a serious disadvantage compared to the multi-laundry firms in terms of transport costs.

If we wanted a long term future we would have to go national, but I was now in my fifties and not at all sure that was the road for me. Quite apart from which, the cost would be considerable and would certainly require a dilution of my shareholding to raise sufficient capital. I was aware that my being the sole shareholder (not strictly true—Judy held a few) was something the bank saw as a minus, and there would be a distinct limit to the number of eggs they would put into a one-man basket! This question of dilution was something I had refused to consider right from the time all the shares in the company fell to me. So many businesses I had bought had gone down the tubes because of family or shareholder infighting, and there was no way that was going to happen during my period of office, added to which the shares had now acquired a certain value, and under the fiscal regime of the time could only be passed on to the next generation with severe tax implications. More particularly in the last decade, there had been much interest in us from the quoted sector. These requests we always agreed to explore, getting sometimes as far as preliminary negotiations, but never pressing to a conclusion. But there is a time and tide in the affairs of men, and my ground was shifting.

I have always been a passionate supporter of capitalism as the only effective form of wealth creation yet devised. The only serious alternative, the centrally controlled economies of communism, just couldn't deliver acceptable results—the end product being that the countries so governed had uniformly wretched living standards for the vast majority. However, capitalism had one big problem—not enough people were capitalists!

In essence capitalism is an expression of energy—wealth creating energy. Like all forms of energy, however, it must be controlled and directed for it to be of value to mankind. Earthquakes, hurricanes and tornados, explosives, nuclear fission—all these are in themselves uncontrolled, large scale energy, and can do a great deal of damage. Yet all have the potential, if harnessed, to be forces for good. Capitalism similarly, if controlled and directed, is an immense and beneficial power, able to benefit all who come within its orbit. In the last one hundred years much progress has been made to do just this. Beginning with the Anti Trust Laws in the States and the Monopolies Commission here, a large body of legislation is in being, and from time to time extended, to achieve just that control.

As of now there is no serious contender to capitalism. Communism and socialism have both been widely tested and, quite simply, failed to deliver. Today, even the two great heartlands of the communist wealth creating system, Russia and China, have abandoned it, or are in the process of doing so. The very few countries still holding out, such as Cuba and North Korea, are in a disastrous condition, the consequences of which are being picked up by their peoples.

Most want to see ongoing improvements to schools, health services, transport in all its forms, law enforcement, and much else. All have one requirement in common—money is needed to realise the aim. For sufficient money to be available for these laudable aims requires that the wealth creating power of the community be sufficiently robust to allow large sums to be filtered out for these purposes. To print and spend a pound that is not supported by an equivalent amount of new wealth is self-defeating. Governments do try from time to time, but always their efforts are subject to an ineluctable and corrective law. It's called inflation. Whenever there arises a mismatch between real wealth creation and the money supply, inflation is the automatic mechanism that will correct the imbalance. No government can stop it, no union can overcome it, no company can halt it. There is no short cut to funds being available for desirable objectives, only genuine wealth creation, and capitalism is the proven and most efficient vehicle for that purpose.

The first step on the road to making every man a capitalist is to enable him to buy, and become the owner of his home. We had taken steps to make this a reality for our people. So, what next? Logically, acquiring an equity stake in the company he worked for. That began an extended study into the pros and cons of such a move. I contacted a firm called 'Job Ownership Ltd', the driving force of which was a man called Robert Oakeshott. He had an almost evangelical zeal for the principle of workers owning equity, and I learnt much from him.

In the event there were very real obstacles. The first was taxation. In its wisdom, the then Labour government had introduced legislation, the effect of which was to render all transfers of equity taxable. The idea was to stop family businesses being passed down the generations. This however applied to employees just as much as sons or daughters. Given Labour's philosophy, this effect was almost certainly something they had not taken into the reckoning. An illustration of the law of unintended consequences! Nonetheless, it was the law of the land. In our case that would have resulted in a heavy tax demand that could only have been met by the company. This in turn must have damaged its competitive place in the market—a serious minus.

Then, when looking closely at how such an equity distribution scheme would work in practice, there were other problems. Beneficial ownership by an employee raises the question, what happens when he leaves the company or dies? He will sell his shares or maybe pass them on to his offspring who, in all likelihood, won't work for the company whose shares they are. In one generation, therefore, the business is back to the situation where one set of people owns the shares, while another works in the firm.

An alternative is for there to be an arrangement whereby the company buys back the shares at market value when the holder retires or leaves. This, in due time, must pose a heavy drain on the company finances, again with its impact on competitiveness. A third way, the John Lewis Partnership way, is for all the shares to be held in trust, so that no one holds any beneficially. This avoids the drawbacks of the first two approaches, the gain for the individual being their entitlement to a defined share of any profit. In practice, this hardly differs from a conventional business with a sound profit sharing scheme, save that it does stop the top men making a killing on share movements or options.

These were sufficient grounds for me not to proceed, though I did make gifts to my people as indicated elsewhere. To the purist, not a very satisfactory substitute! Had all the other difficulties been resolved, would I have gone ahead and converted the place to a worker owned business? Not an easy question to answer. Over the years I had ploughed everything back into the company, so it was almost all I had. What would have been a possibility was to retain ownership of the building, and rent it to the cooperative had the other obstacles been resolved. This would have had the merit of not leaving me high and dry had the co-operative failed. This, however, is all in the realm of the hypothetical and such are not the most rewarding questions to try and answer.

There was one further stumbling block—management. No business is better than its people, and of those, management is the most important. The worker owned business has significantly greater difficulty attracting high calibre people because of the limitations it places on salaries at the top, and opportunities for personal gain. Quite apart from which, laundries, along with other small businesses, have great difficulty anyway, attracting top-drawer people. It had become clear looking at the whole field of co-operative ventures, that just turning employees into owners would by no means guarantee success. Having taken a look at some that didn't make it, management was a key factor in all of them.

My links with J.O.L and Robert continued and developed. He asked me to join the board, numerically by far the largest board I have ever been involved in! The chairman was Joe Grimond, sometime Liberal party leader, known in the Lords as 'The Sage', a delightfully genuine chap with a slightly world-weary air. Sitting round the table there were a couple of very reasonable senior union officials; also Sam Britten (brother of Leon) who for many years was a financial journalist, writing for, among others, the *F. T.* He had a very able mind, but tended to assume that what he said would be treated as gospel. And a little aggrieved when it wasn't! Also David Young, at that time finance director of the John Lewis Partnership—a very sound man, though I recall being surprised at how firm, even harsh, were the disciplinary procedures taken against defaulting 'partners'. There were several other luminaries. I'm not sure how much I was able to contribute, but learnt much.

One of life's coincidences was finding Philip Baxendale also a board member. It was from Philip I had bought the Chorley Briggs Laundry over a decade earlier. Philip did convert his engineering business to a worker owned company. It was a substantial affair employing some seven hundred people. Sadly, the whole thing has unravelled. At the time, a block was put on any share sales by the beneficiaries for five years. As soon as the five-year moratorium was up, a depressingly large percentage of the work force sold. Since which time, there has been further erosion of the principle concept, that the man who worked there also owned a share.

In the post one morning was a letter from a Mike Kemp who asked if he could visit—he was interested in buying a laundry. On the premise that you never say 'no' on day one, he was invited and duly arrived, though did say he almost turned round when he saw the place, it was so obviously far beyond his pocket. Before leaving, he mentioned that he had a friend whom he felt sure would be acutely interested, and who was currently chairman of a small quoted company called Charles Baynes. Could he arrange for him to come? Again, on the same premise, he came. The chap was a Peter Dellar who had made a lot of money, sold up, and went to eat grapes on a Bermuda beach. Finding himself quickly bored to death, he decided to get back into the commercial world, specifically laundries, of which he had previous experience. He was looking for one to set the ball rolling, his intention being to build a national chain. He had never seen anything like our place in the laundry world, was very obviously fired up, and determined to conclude a deal if he could—a state of affairs that helped me materially in the negotiations!

Discussions began and a deal reached. Accountants came in to do their 'due diligence', found nothing amiss, and the lawyers were set to reduce it all to writing. Just before the agreement went solid, an opportunity arose to buy one of the very few remaining private laundries on Merseyside. It was a natural for us, but because we were on the verge of transferring ownership, it was right to involve Peter. I told him of the position, and sought his view. He also recognised that it was an obvious 'must', but, he told me later, he sat on the edge of his seat waiting to see if I would ask for an increase in the agreed price on the grounds of a material change. His tension was due to the fact that he desperately wanted to complete the deal, but had already gone further than the city thought prudent, and couldn't go any higher! However, we had reached a deal, had shaken hands on it, and such matters are to be honoured. A very fair price was on the table and it was that which formed the basis of the transaction that took place in a London office on the 23rd December 1983.

It was a time of mixed emotions, but there were one or two distinctly pleasurable moments. False modesty (my wife says modesty of any sort!) has never burdened me, and I am very clear that the deciding factor in any business is always the party in control, normally the chairman or chief executive. He is the one man in the company whose decisions will make or break it. All of this fully allowed, he can't run the thing by himself—he is dependent on the people round him actually to deliver the results. If he doesn't have any people, or if he doesn't have the right people, he soon doesn't have a business. It therefore seemed appropriate to include our folk in the fruits of the sale. They had been loyal and fully supportive.

All employees on the books on the day of the sale got a minimum of £1,000 (part timers £500) ranging up to a few thousands for those with longer service. Management received £7,500 each, my sister a six-figure sum and my mother an annuity that added substantially to her income. We even found a way of getting the money across to them mostly free of tax. For the children I set up a six-figure Trust fund—this to be used for any worthwhile project.

Christmas that year was a time of some reflection. The family were now grown to adulthood, or nearly so. Mark had got a respectable mechanical engineering degree at Imperial and had returned to the company that had sponsored him, Tube Investments. Anne had completed her training as a state registered nurse at Barts. She was by this time functioning at the sharp end of the hospital world. Later she was to specialise in oncology, a particularly demanding form of nursing that required those involved to keep a careful grip on themselves. Richard was reading law at Peterhouse, Cambridge, with a view to securing an LL.B. And Mandy was halfway through her A levels at Rugby school, having opted to board there. There were no headaches with the children—all were making steady progress. Judy, once the children were all grown, had taken a job as a medical social worker and found it rewarding.

For my own part, I found myself looking back over some thirty-four years that had passed like an evening gone. It had all proved to be intensely satisfying and I had loved my commercial life. In retrospect, even the crises, for whilst it is absolutely right to aim always for the plusses in this life, it is the minuses that are the making of us. Holding the entire share capital had given me a freedom of action that was very precious; it meant I could use the company as a platform for experiment in a way that, had there been other shareholders, would probably not have been possible.

There had come a moment when a company, with a full stock market quote called Provincial Laundries, approached me with an invitation to reverse Cleggs into their business. They had experienced serious management weaknesses and believed we could resolve them. I was to be chairman of the enlarged operation and hold a large block of shares, though less than 51%. Provincial were about three times our size, so it would have been very difficult to argue that we should hold the majority. The discussions foundered on my recognising that my freedom of action would be, in some measure, compromised. This was a watershed and forced me to accept that we would have to grow much more slowly as a private company, compared with the possibilities offered by a publicly quoted one.

In the event, Provincial was bought by one Ashcroft. He turned out to he an exceptionally astute businessman who today is a billionaire, has given the Tory party millions, and in exchange got himself a peerage! Perhaps I missed the boat! Still, for me, to be head of a mouse was better than to be tail of a lion, though the smart guys, the Ashcrofts of this world, manage to be head of a lion!

Nothing is forever in this world or, as Ecclesiastes so succinctly puts it, "There is a time to begin and a time to end." December 23rd 1983 was both an ending and a beginning. It was time to move on to that new beginning.

A NEW BEGINNING

At the time of the sale I had no clear plans for the future, but at 53 certainly did not want to put my feet up. Peter Dellar had tried it and found it impossible. My resolve was simply that if something emerged where I felt I might be able to make a contribution, I would have a go. One was not long in coming. Pilkingtons had formed an organisation called the St. Helen's Community Trust, in response to burgeoning unemployment in the town, as their world beating invention called 'float glass' led to much lower numbers of employees. The Trust was to become the model for the government's subsequent 'Enterprise Trusts', and which were set up across the nation. The director of the Trust, David Boult, rang and asked me to go and help them; they particularly needed people with a business background. The role fitted like a glove, and was to lead to some interesting, not to say hair-raising, moments.

Before this, however, and very shortly after the sale of the company to Baynes Plc, though not part of the agreement, the chairman asked me to join his board as a non-executive. This had particular appeal; it meant keeping close to events in my old company and watching its progress, as well as the development of the larger business. In the light of events, 'progress' might not be the most appropriate word, but that is to anticipate. Board meetings were in Cardiff where the company had its head office.

The chairman was a wine buff, and ran a small business in fine wines, all of which were stored in the capacious cellars beneath his offices. He took me down there on a couple of occasions. It was an Aladdin's Cave of wine—all the best years (except 1945) of the great classified wines. He kept only French and had all the first growths. Having for the first time in my life some spare cash, it seemed an appropriate moment to buy about forty cases, a dozen or more of which are still in my cellar!

Peter is a free spirit, and proved to be too much of a wheeler-dealer to settle to the strict disciplines essential to the proper discharge of the office of chairman, particularly of a public company. Within little more than three years he had quit under pressure from the city. In the few years prior to the sale, Cleggs had averaged a profit of £250k. (circa. £600k in current money). Two years later it had moved into loss, due to the wrong man going in as general manager, and filling the place with cheap work. Non-executives can only ask questions and advise, they cannot execute.

We had never moved house since marrying and building our first home, twenty-six years previously. At that time all we had were our wedding presents, and a few other items that had been collected in anticipation. It was a home in which we had been very happy, in which the children had grown up, and indeed in which two of them had been born. It was however just five minutes walk from the new factory. Too close for comfort—there was quite a lot of me in that place. We agreed that if somewhere suitable could be found within about a thirty-five mile radius, we would move. Notifying two or three agents and indicating the acceptable parameters, the hunt began. Expensively produced and very glossy brochures started to pour through the letterbox, some bearing little relationship to the advised criteria! Sifting through them, about one in seven seemed to justify a visit. If the camera doesn't lie, it also doesn't tell the whole truth! Gardens and rooms can be made to look larger than they really are, and the local electricity pylon carefully excluded from view!

Of those we did go to see, the owners were invariably helpful and pleasant, offered coffee and gave freedom to roam. It could be a little difficult accepting such kindly hospitality when, within two minutes, we knew the place wasn't for us. A deep recession was just ending, and houses were not moving that readily. Then a call came from Jackson Stops, one of the agents we had contacted, to say a place was coming on the market for which the brochure had not yet been printed, but which they felt sure, from what we had indicated, that it would be of interest. It was a sometime rectory in a place called Gawsworth, and which was just about within our distance range. Within seconds of seeing it we agreed it was right for us. A phone call to Stops at their Chester office on arriving home offered them the asking price in full. The contact there was a Graham Adnitt, a senior partner.

Thus began a negotiating roundabout. Mr Adnitt said he would communicate my offer to his client. My response was that the sum offered was that sought, and all that was necessary was to proceed to contract. Not so. Ten days later the advice was that the offer was insufficient and would we care to increase it? Increased it was. Another ten days, and the same again. A third time, and yet again. Clearly the agents had two or three other interested parties, and were going the rounds doing a Dutch auction. After the third increase I told the agents, that was it—anymore and they would have to find it elsewhere. However, by this time I had met the owner and discovered that he was very anxious to convalesce at the

Old Rectory following a major operation for cancer. Linked with my final offer was a willingness to let him fill in his own completion date, provided contracts were exchanged without further delay.

This may well have proved decisive, for contracts were exchanged in July while completion was in December! The delay was of no great moment—we had a home to live in, and it gave time for my architect and builders to get themselves organised for the works that were needed before we moved in. They began work the day after the previous owners, the Owens, left, and completed the jobs in May the following year. There had been substantial remedial and modification works needed.

Adnitt was surprised that I didn't want a surveyor's report before exchanging contracts. Firstly, the house had been around for over five hundred years and would therefore probably see our time out! More seriously, any report, given the age of the place, would be so hedged about with qualifications as to be of very little worth, save the better to protect the surveyor from any claims against later discovered flaws. The most common reason for a surveyor's report is to give the purchaser a weapon to beat the vendor down on price. With others waiting in the wings such was not likely to prove effective in this case.

Soaked in history, the original part was built in 1470, with additions to the rear in 1870. A church property until the 1950's, it has been continuously occupied. A typical Cheshire, black and white long house, timber framed, with wattle and daub infill, and now listed Grade 1, it is good for another five hundred plus years with reasonable stewardship. The great hall, one of very few still remaining in Cheshire, is intact, and retains much that was in being when the place was first built. No kings, queens or famous people have ever slept there, but it has witnessed a vast number of the seminal events of our country. Because it was a church property until the mid-twentieth century, and the church kept good records, every incumbent whose home it was is listed.

My sister was looking also to move. A part of the Old Rectory had earlier been formed into what is effectively a self-contained section. We had no use for it, not planning to have any live-in butlers or whatever! It is spacious, has two bedrooms, and most of it is part of the original 1470 structure. She accepted the offer to set up home there. The children, on the other hand, had largely fled the nest by this time. Only Mandy, the youngest, was still based with us, and she only for a few more years. This didn't stop Judy from naming a bedroom for each of them!

One of Judy's requirements in any house we bought was that it must have not less than six bedrooms. Given we were down to ourselves and Mandy, and she not likely to be permanent, this seemed a bit unnecessary. Judy was adamant; we needed them for the grandchildren. But we didn't have any grandchildren; none of the children were even married! Judy was right—marriages there were, and grandchildren followed, all eleven! There are times when six bedrooms are insufficient!

An invitation to serve on the board of a private hospital based in St. Helens had been accepted about a year before finishing at Cleggs. The chairman was an old friend from our bachelor days, David Pilkington. The hospital had been started, as were so many things in the town, by Pilkingtons, the glass company. It began as a nursing home, primarily for ex-Pilkington employees, but had not proved successful. It was about this time that Mrs Barbara Castle, who was then Health Secretary in the Labour government, stopped all private wards in the N.H.S. It gave the kiss of life to the private sector, and so Fairfield was turned into an acute hospital. In the days following Mrs Castle's ban, the demand for private hospital services ballooned far beyond the immediate ability of the sector to meet. It was a licence to print money! As always in such situations, supply will rise to meet demand, and today the private hospital world is intensely competitive. Mrs Castle's objective was to get rid of all self-funded health care, in the event she kick-started private health provision into a massive expansion—another classic illustration of the 'law of unintended consequences'. She did achieve, however, the removal from the N.H.S. of a useful source of income.

Fairfield Hospital was a rewarding company to be linked with. It was young, thrusting and very well run. The hospital management team was led by Mrs Margaret Greenall, a nurse of long standing, who proved also to have a strong entrepreneurial streak. She was a natural businesswoman. The company was a registered charity, so the rewarding bit was wholly job satisfaction, payment not being allowed to directors of charities! When David retired, I became chairman and remained so for the following five plus years until reaching the company's compulsory retirement age of seventy. It was the company's good fortune, when Margaret retired, to have a very able successor in John Williams who had previously been the Finance Executive.

One of the highlights, during my period as chairman, was the winning of the British Safety Council's 'Sword of Honour'. Fairfield was the first hospital in the U.K. to win this, either private or N.H.S. We won it a second time the following year. It was through this that I got to know Sir Ned Purvis who was running the B.S.C. at that time. Ned had served much of his sea time in nuclear submarines, where operational safety is a way of life. In time he became an admiral and Third Sea Lord. He knew Vice Admiral Sir David Brown very well, my sometime cadet captain on H.M.S. Conway, with whom, after a long gap, I had recently renewed contact.

I had, of course, been on the board of Charles Baynes Plc., one of whose divisions specialised in high integrity valves. This division supplied all the valve requirements of British nuclear submarines and Ned was very familiar with Charles Baynes! These valves were assembled and finished in 'clean room' conditions and to the most stringent standards. So we had much to talk about and shared some enjoyable meals.

By now Mark had completed his studies at Imperial College, gained a respectable degree in mechanical engineering, and completed his stint with his sponsors, Tube Investments. His ambition was to have his own engineering company and in due time used his share of the money from the fund I had set up for the children, to help finance it. Anne had married, and had her wedding reception on the lawn of the Old Rectory in a marquee. She too had claimed her share of the fund, this time to set up home in London where they bought a flat. Richard too had ended his time at Peterhouse with a very good degree. Now an LL.B, he was doing time at law school in Guildford. Mandy was nearing the end of her school days and would shortly be leaving Rugby for Manchester University where she would read English, the same subject and the same university as her mother. One of the students in Judy's day would be one of Mandy's lecturers! Richard had also claimed his share of the fund to set up home in West Hampstead. Later, Mandy set up home in Windsor and that saw the end of the fund.

One day at the Community Trust, David Boult asked if I would go with the two owners of a business to a meeting with their bank, a meeting that promised to be difficult. It was scheduled for the following day, so I spent most of the intervening time getting up to speed with their affairs and being briefed on the situation. The company were specialist roofing contractors, aiming at the prestige end of the market, and using a patented German system. It was an outstanding product of very high quality. The most visible example of the work done by the company is the roof of the modernistic R.A.C. building adjacent to the East side of the M.6, close to Birmingham and not far from the No.9 intersection.

The business had been a 'start up' a couple of years previously, and was a perfect example of the 'J' curve cashflow problem. A 'start up' situation involves cash being laid out for a variety of needs, the return on which will, if all goes well, be sometime in the middle future. Then, in the early stages, when business is won, more cash goes out than comes in. The more business, the worse it gets. That is the downward part of the J. Then, assuming the business is well run and the numbers have been properly crunched, there comes a point when incoming cash exceeds outgoing, which is the rising arm of the J.

The bank's position was that they had used up all their facilities, and they were not willing to provide any more. More damaging, promises had been given which had not been kept relating to the timing of an improvement in the over-draft position. Businesses that want a long-term future should not make promises to their bank that they cannot keep. Not only is it the fact of a broken promise, bad enough in itself, but also indicates that the entrepreneurs are not fully in con-trol of their affairs. And without more cash the business would fold. The bank had called the meeting to inform the shareholders that they were putting it into receivership.

On studying the figures, the order book, the debtors and creditors, the com-pletion dates of orders in being, etc., it seemed to me that the business really was at the bottom of the curve and about to turn up. When, having listened to all the arguments, it was clear that the bank was not to he moved, I finally offered to guarantee a sufficient part of the overdraft for them to back off. They adjourned the meeting till the following day whilst they checked out whether my guarantee was acceptable. It was, and the company survived. The bank asked that I should become chairman, and this was accepted by the two entrepreneurs.

In the way of these things, my assessment of the underlying position on this occasion, proved correct. Almost immediately, cashflow became positive and good profits were to be generated in the coming months and years. Despite the fact that in those early stages my only real contribution had been to read the runes correctly, the bank gave me all the credit! Justice is a very approximate quantity in this world! It may not come as a surprise that within a week, monthly management accounts had been set up!

It wasn't long before the bank was in touch to say that they had another com-pany in difficulties, and would I care to take a look? It is possible to feel almost sorry for banks at times. Whatever may be said to the contrary, banks don't enjoy putting companies down. They make money from live businesses, not dead ones. They do, however, have strict criteria for lending, and when those are materially breached they have a problem. They can't pretend the situation doesn't exist. Neither can they sort out the business themselves. They can, and do, call for an accountant's report, which for a small company only adds to the difficulty because they are left to pick up a fairly hefty bill. Often the report doesn't solve much; it perhaps helps the bank to say "we did all we could". It is into such situ-ations that such as myself may have a part to play.

By this time we had moved to Gawsworth, and settled in to this lovely old house. The garden needed a lot of work, it having been neglected. My sister, who had moved into her part as soon as completion in December, was a keen gardener and began, with the aid of a full time man we had inherited, to pull it round. He clearly hadn't been used to working quite so energetically, and didn't survive very long! He was replaced by two part-timers who gave us some hours a week each. Inside, the furniture from Rainhill left a lot of empty spaces, so there began a programme of acquisition, beginning with the purchase of several items from the previous owner. Curtains and carpets had been organised before we moved in. Part of the alterations involved adding two more bathrooms, to turn two bedrooms into self-contained suites, ideal for guests.

Despite the very considerable works that were completed in the six months prior to moving in, there remained a great deal to be done. So a chap who had been on my company's books for a number of years, and whose line was fabric maintenance, agreed to work steadily through a long list at weekends. Working about forty weekends a year for the next several years, he finally completed everything. With a house of this age, though, there is always something to he done, and it is important to keep on top of repairs and maintenance.

Richard duly completed his articles and became a fully-fledged lawyer, moving to a small firm in Hampstead. It was around this time that he met Graham who had spent time in the States and in Australia. Graham is a gentle giant who stands six foot five in his socks! It has proved a durable relationship, whilst his link with the leisure industry has done nothing to diminish the remarkable collection of distant places they have visited. Anne had qualified as an S.R.N., and was busy nursing in between having her five children. Mark was running his engineering business and Mandy got a very good degree at Manchester in English. She decided to take up journalism, passed her exams with flying colours, and won a couple of prizes which yielded a few hundred pounds!

The family were well launched. Anne had married Chris, her schoolboy sweetheart. They had met at Rugby school, and from that moment on she didn't look at anyone else. Mark had fallen for a girl he had met, and they were shortly to marry. Alison is a lawyer who for a number of years worked for Clifford Chance, where she was very highly thought of. In between she managed to produce three fine boys. Mark's business was near Luton so they settled in St. Albans, where they still remain.

The company that R.B.S. had asked me to look at was called Holroyd Meek Ltd. It was a 'start up' by two energetic school chums who had spent time in the distribution side of the catering world. The driving force was Bill Holroyd. The business was the supply to multiple restaurants of all their catering needs. This meant they had to be able to handle ambient, chilled and frozen foods.

When I first became involved, the office was a rather tired portokabin and some inexpensive storage, rented by the square foot. They had one lorry. The difference that was to emerge between this distribution company and the many look-alikes, was that Bill had an idea. All the others who had warehousing facilities bought in their product and sold it on with a mark-up, plus a charge for the distribution. They were getting two bites of the cherry and the client never knew what the true distribution charge was, because it was taken up with the sale of the goods. Bill said to his clients: "You decide the product you want, negotiate the best price you can with the supplier; we will then buy that product from that supplier on your behalf and invoice it out to you at the price you have agreed with them. We will then charge for the distribution to your outlets, and make our profit from that." This at once meant the client knew his transport costs exactly, and had complete freedom to buy his supplies from wherever he wanted, and at the best price he could negotiate. It was a winning formula.

The problem from the bank's point of view was that old one of overtrading. It is probably the biggest single cause of bankruptcies in the commercial world. Bill was getting business faster than his cash resources could handle, and the strain was being taken at the bank. And the bank wasn't happy. At their suggestion Bill and Andy Meek agreed to meet me, and that was the beginning of a friendship that still endures. The chemistry was right and we got on well. In time I joined the board and for a short period was acting chairman.

It was a great company, though in retrospect I seemed to spend most of my time trying to slow the rate of growth. Many times I found myself saying to Bill, "William, you are expanding this business into bankruptcy!" (For some reason I always called him William, never Bill!) The growth was phenomenal. In short order, brand new purpose-built warehousing was up and running, and the one lorry became dozens. Turnover soared to millions, then scores of millions, then hundreds of millions. Two, quarter million square feet warehouses were built, one in the North West, the other in the Midlands, and more lorries.

Bill started his working day at about 5-00 a.m., and finished when the job was done, perhaps about 6-00 p.m. or later. From the office he would go to the gym for a vigorous workout! He had tremendous energy and a bubbling enthusiasm. He commanded the total loyalty of his hard-pressed management team. No matter how much he demanded of them, he always gave more of himself.

By this time he was a major player in the specialised area of distribution in which he operated, and the competition were having to come to terms with his approach and began to copy it. Some of these were very large, and financially powerful, quoted firms. Holroyd Meek was privately owned by a handful of shareholders, myself by this time being one. It was time to sell, and there were those very willing to buy. With the help of Rothschilds, a very good deal was completed with Bookers (they of the book prize fame). A condition of the purchase was that the board of H.M. joined Bookers distribution board for not less than two years.

This was not a rewarding time. The then chief executive had recently been recruited to try and sort out a sprawling, ill controlled business, which had lost whatever focus it may once have had. A likeable man in himself, he lacked an adequate grasp of the job, and didn't survive very long, but long enough to acquire H.M. In the short term the acquisition made things worse. There had been no coherent logic in the purchase, and little thought had been given to how it would fit. As soon as my minimum period was up I resigned, as did Bill. A year or two later, Booker was taken over and is today part of the 'Big Food Group'. The jury is still out on whether they have got a real grip on their affairs.

Around the middle eighties Mrs Thatcher introduced a thing called Business Expansion Scheme. When she first came to power the top rate of tax was 98%. Whether this should more accurately be called theft rather than tax would make a fine philosophical debate! Initially this was reduced to 80% and it was at that level when the B.E.S. provisions were introduced. These allowed for up to £40k to be relieved of tax, provided the money was put into an approved scheme of high-risk investments. The thinking behind the scheme was that historically, most successful companies had grown from very small beginnings financed from established wealth. Taxation throughout the post-war years had been at levels that had eroded the capacity of individuals to take the high levels of risk that are inevitable with new businesses. If the money wasn't put into the scheme, the party concerned would pay £32k in tax on his £40k. Effectively therefore he was really risking only £8k., with the possibility that he might back a winner.

The St. Helens Trust decided to form a B.E.S. fund, appealing to wealthy local people to try and offset unemployment in the area. This had begun to rise as coalmines started closing. I was asked to become chairman of the investment panel, consisting of just myself and three other experienced businessmen. It was our task to decide which applications for funds were potentially viable. Almost all were start-ups and therefore involved very high risk.

It was a fascinating job, and one that taught quite a lot about human nature! We quickly established some ground rules. Firstly, the entrepreneur had to contribute some equity, and therefore had himself to be at risk. There are multitudes that will take money if someone else is carrying all the risk! Secondly, business plan, cashflow and P. & L. projections, and 'worst case' scenarios were a must, and often the Trust itself would help in their preparation. Such is the optimism of the would-be businessman that we usually found the 'worst case' turned out to be the 'best case', and sometimes not even that!

The two critical areas were market and man. Did he have a realistic chance of breaking into the market against established competition? To have a reasonable chance of success meant being able to offer a comparable product at lower cost, or an improved one at the same price. Only if persuaded that the market potential was there did we get to the next stage. Given the market exists, the entrepreneur is the key. Has he got what it takes? The energy, drive, resilience in the face of problems, willingness to work as long as it takes, with initially perhaps little reward? These were the sort of qualities we were looking for. How to accurately assess the applicant? A good question! No doubt being God would help!

Our average investment was in the £30k–£50k range, in today's money about £60k–£100k. in some half dozen companies a year. How well did they perform? We got more wrong than right! It seldom took more than one or two years, and sometimes not even that to sort out the men from the boys. About one in three or four really performed, with an occasional splendid winner. But this was an area of venture capitalism where one success will pay for up to half a dozen failures. Of the five years we ran the scheme, one was very successful and returned to the investors not only their original money but a useful profit on top. This when anything over an £8k return on a £40k investment meant a paper gain! My recollection is that in each year we produced a result that made it worthwhile to have invested, though often it was only the tax relief that made it so.

As levels of taxation fell year by year to their present level of 40% it became harder to persuade people to put their money into what was always recognised as a high-risk area. The lower top rate tax became the more the individual was putting at risk. At 40% tax, £24k was being risked, a much larger number. No matter, there are a number of businesses in the St. Helens area which are today creating wealth and jobs as a result of the scheme.

The Trust's initiative was probably unique in that it was able to operate a fund that was much smaller than would have been viable in a national scheme, this because all those involved gave their time without charge. Also the Revenue identified us as working within the spirit of the tax provisions, and once a year a high level official came to discuss with us how the thing could be improved and made more effective. It is perhaps inevitably the case that some of the best minds in the country, whenever tax legislation is amended to make possible something like

B.E.S., are immediately bent to finding ways of turning it to advantage—in this case by finding low-risk investments that still qualified for relief. We didn't—all our funds went to precisely the areas intended.

G.M. meanwhile had prospered, despite the strained relations between the two founding entrepreneurs. These strains reached breaking point when one of them, Mullins, the M. bit of G.M., walked out. It was all very acrimonious, but understandable. The two chaps, Guest and Mullins, were very different characters, and approached the business from widely separated standpoints. To add a further highly inflammable ingredient to this, Mullins married Guest's sometime wife. Bill Guest had no problems with Keith Mullins taking his ex-wife—he rather took the view he was more than welcome to her! But, of course, the children went with the mother, and Bill's children meant much to him. In the sphere of interpersonal relations, this was the most difficult business in which I ever became involved. Mullins leaving was a problem in some ways, but a positive relief in others. Sadly, he died within a year or so of his departure.

One of the fundamental differences between them was that Keith always took a short-term view of everything, Bill a much longer term. This, in the running of a business, must lead to starkly opposed positions on matters such as investment and the direction of the company. It was only after Keith had died that I wondered whether, at some sub-conscious level, he had a premonition that he was not destined to longevity.

At a purely practical level, the business continued to move ahead. Larger premises were bought, and these thoroughly overhauled. They included an excellent drawing office and ample space. Bill grew into the job, and was a new man without the Mullins factor grinding away like sand in an oyster. Good business was won, and the profits followed. G.M. was nearly always a sub-contractor to a large national and publicly quoted company. They won the order, and G.M. was contracted to do the roofing. The average value of a G.M. contract was about a million pounds. Relations with the main contractors, all household names, were invariably good.

In time a recession overtook the commercial building sector and hit it very hard. The main contractors at once began to pass the pain down the line. G.M. having put in an interim monthly invoice for work done during the period, the main contractor began to find fault, either trivial or fantasy. A cheque for say 30% of the value of the invoice would be received and an invitation to discuss the rest. Virtually all the main contractors, as if in concert, began the same practice. G.M's debtor list ballooned out of control. The company had a choice—it could walk off the job with possibly serious implications, it could appeal to a body that would take many months to reach a finding, or it could try and exploit its earlier good relations to reach a workable solution. It sought the last, but failed, and had finally to ask the receivers in.

It was a sad end to a sound and once thriving business. It became clear, as the main contractors reported their own results, which were uniformly appalling, and some close to the edge themselves, that survival had been the name of the game. They were aware of G.M's size and that they were not fiscally strong enough to survive the tactics adopted. The receivers later told Bill that they had succeeded in getting only about fifteen percent of the several millions of the debtor list paid. Those were the millions that aided all the main contractors' survival. It is a rough, tough world when the chips are down.

R.B.S. meanwhile had asked me to look at several other companies. One, with the rather exotic name of Royal Staffordshire, was a manufacturer of china and porcelain products, based in Burslem. It seemed an interesting possibility so I agreed to have a look. The look didn't last very long. The world of fine bone china is an esoteric one that can best he described as a black art! The company had state of the art ovens for firing the product, but it still mattered which way the wind blew! It didn't take long for me to advise the bank that there was nothing that I could usefully contribute.

Another was a printing company whose name escapes me. My chief recollection was that the husband and wife team, whose business it was, had ambitions of grandeur considerably ahead of their ability to deliver the necessary support. These ambitions were non negotiable. Anything I advised that clashed with the number one priority, was unacceptable. There was little option but again to pull out. This last always gave pause; my involvement was inevitably a last effort by the bank to do something to save the business. Pulling out had to mean the end of the line, and not something I ever felt able to do lightly.

The company that bought me, Charles Baynes, also lost its direction under Peter Dellar and he came under pressure from the city to go. He went, though Judy and I have remained in touch with him and his lovely wife, Jill. Peter is a likeable and resilient chap who will never rust. Since leaving Baynes he has pursued a wide range of interests and businesses, both here and overseas.

His successor, Dr. Bruce McInnes, was a very different character. Bruce is a South African who had begun life as a university lecturer, his doctorate being in chemistry. In due time he found himself rescuing a defunct company called Hudeco and did a remarkable job. By this time he had also qualified as a chartered accountant, decided there was no real future in South Africa, and came over to England where his reputation as a successful businessman stood him in good stead.

Peter told me I would be expected to resign, and so I gave him a signed, undated, letter of resignation. To my surprise, Bruce called in at Gawsworth and asked me to remain on the board. This might have owed something to the fact I was holding a useful number of shares, which would be more likely to be kept if I remained a board member!

For the next several years I had the privilege of seeing the best manager of my commercial lifetime at work. He ran a tight, extremely well ordered ship, the way a business should be run, and the company prospered under his direction. Initially, after Bruce took over, I was almost the only English national round the table, for Bruce brought over his tried and tested team from South Africa. The laundry division was sold on, so my much diminished contact with my old company was finally lost completely. I remained on his board until the retirement age of 65, did an extra year at his request, and that ended one more chapter.

Baynes has since been delisted, having been turned into an unquoted company. Bruce has himself moved over to the private sector, forming a new business from scratch, confirming what he had said to me years earlier, that he envied the chairman's comparative freedom in an unlisted company. This was a brave thing to do; new start up companies are the highest risk area of all in the commercial world. Bruce being Bruce, however, is its best guarantee of success! My latest information is that his business has moved into profit. We have remained good friends, have kept in touch, and link up around one or more times a year.

By now there had been considerable family development. Mark and Alison had three boys. Anne and Chris had four girls and a boy, and Mandy and Tom would in due course produce two boys and a girl. Mandy had met Tom through his sister and it developed into a romance. Tom had also been to Rugby school, but Mandy and he never met there. It seems that school has played a major role in the affairs of our family. Our four children were educated there, both our sons-in-law were, and Anne and Chris have two of their children there at the moment, one girl and the boy, with the prospect of a third one in the offing. Mandy and Tom's daughter Sarah has also expressed a wish to go. There should be a discount for quantity!

Mark's engineering business folded. It was a sector that had not had the easiest of rides in recent years, but in addition Mark's strength was in sales and marketing, and he never quite got a grip on the business as a whole. Much was left to subordinates without adequate controls to oversee them. It was a difficult period for him, his self-confidence took a severe jolt, and it took time to recover. However, he dusted himself down, began consultancy work, and in due time was offered and accepted the position of operations director in a Swedish quoted company making medical equipment. Recently he has moved back into a privately owned engineering company, having agreed an equity stake. This time, however, his role is limited to sales and marketing, involving the E.U. as well as the U.K.

Anne moved over to the commercial world, started her own residential estate agency, and has gone from strength to strength. She now has a payroll of some thirty or more and is expanding steadily. Her husband is a chartered surveyor who started his own business a number of years previously, specialising in the commercial side, so the two complement each other. The thing that pushed Anne out of nursing was simply that five children and hospital hours just didn't gel. She has proved to be commercially astute; this, combined with her very considerable drive and energy, has ensured a highly successful business.

Richard and Graham decided to see whether Australia was the right place to be. With no children to consider, uprooting was not so onerous, and they both found employment in their respective disciplines very quickly. Richard spent much of his time working on the legal aspect of the Sydney Olympics. Finally they came to the conclusion that, whilst Sydney had a lot going for it, it was rather a long way from the centre of gravity, particularly from the commercial world, and Richard was a solicitor specialising in commercial work. Returning to London, Graham joined Cathy Pacific, whilst Richard set up his own practice, took in a partner after about a year, and now has half a dozen assistant solicitors and growing. To accommodate a steadily increasing number of people they have moved three times, and now operate out of an attractive suite of offices of some 10,000 sq.ft., occupying two floors. The upper one is presently sub-let until hoped for expansion calls it into use. Apart from the Australian interlude, Richard has been my solicitor since he qualified.

Before they returned, however, I boarded a German container ship and set sail for Sydney. It was a forty-day trip, with only very brief stops in Rotterdam, Hamburg, La Spezia, Suez and Melbourne. There were only four other passengers and a crew of just eighteen. This last was something of an eye opener for me. Fifty years previously, on a ship a third the size, we had a crew of about sixty-five! Travel by cargo boat is a very different business from a cruise ship. It helps to be self sufficient—no entertainment is provided. The odds against finding a soul mate among the other passengers are considerable when there are only four to choose from! Having prior awareness of all this, I went well supplied with a small library of books, and read the lot.

A great deal had changed since my days at sea. The captain was indistinguishable from his crew—no uniform, no gold braid, just jeans and a sweat shirt! As the voyage continued, I got to know him quite well. He spoke good English. Asking him why he didn't wear a uniform, he said, "When the company pay for it, I will wear it." Plainly, the company were not paying! There was also much apprehension about the infiltration of Phillipino nationals. One such was the third officer, a fact that was bitterly resented by the German officers. He was not allowed to eat in the officers' and passengers' dining room, which seemed to me very unkind. He accepted it all very cheerfully, perhaps sensing that time was on his side. There is no doubt that they represented a threat to the Europeans' futures, for they were willing to work for much lower wages.

The ocean highways are increasingly dominated by third world countries whose crews are being paid a peppercorn compared with the West. Their ships are generally recognisable by their run-down condition. Maintenance and cleanliness are very obviously not the highest priority. None of this prevented my trip from being memorable. The seasickness that had dogged me as a youth was no longer a problem, at least on ocean going vessels.

The ship docked in Sydney at about three in the morning, but Richard and Graham were both there on the quayside. There followed three very enjoyable weeks, which included a brief trip to New Zealand to link up with some friends from years back, the same Keith Lightfoot and his wife Jenny. Then Dean of Hamilton; it was Keith who, many years earlier, had persuaded me to join the Samaritans.

It wasn't long before Mandy and Tom started a family, so journalism had to settle for being part time. Tom runs his own business that is computer based, and links into exhibitions here and abroad, the latter as far as Hong Kong.

Having sold my company I missed the advantages that went with it, the more so as I was still very active in the commercial world. So I formed a small thing called 'Gawsworth Finance Ltd.' With an eye to the future, I made the four children equal shareholders owning 25% each. Any shareholdings I acquired as a result of company involvement were owned by G.F. Having been unimpressed with the way others looked after my funds, from a quite early stage I deployed them through G.F. It didn't take long to discover that backing start up entrepreneurs tended to end in either large profits or large losses! My biggest loss was over £200k and largest gain better than £500k! Taking risk has never caused me to lose sleep—perhaps it should!

Before reclaiming control of my funds from the 'professionals', a further area of risk that at the time seemed to be reasonable, was membership of Lloyds as an underwriting 'name'. On finding myself with funds that needed investing and no longer having a business to put them into, I contacted a firm of financial advisors, Chesham Hill. They teamed me up with a Richard Godfrey-Faussett, whose grandfather, it turned out later, had been an equerry to King George Vth. Sadly, this no doubt prestigious link didn't improve the advice he gave! He it was who suggested Lloyds, pointing out that it was a way of making one's funds work twice. The risk element was downplayed, and indeed Lloyd's names over a period invariably had positive experience. Risk anyway was a way of life for me, so I joined and became a 'name'.

It subsequently emerged that a vigorous recruiting campaign was being conducted, and at its highest point there were some thirty-four thousand names. Within a couple of years it became clear that Lloyds was running into serious trouble. Trading on a reputation built over centuries for absolute probity, they succumbed in the 1980's to greed and corruption. Losses piled up, the old hands had seen what was coming, and saw in the rapid recruitment of new people a way of spreading the pain. It is one thing to support losses made following one's membership. Quite another to he lumbered with losses which the top brass knew were in the pipeline, inevitable, and would surface before long.

Demands for funds to offset these losses began to drop through the letterboxes of most of those thirty-four thousand. In my own case these finally totted up to a million and a half, a number which, had it got to be paid, would have had a material effect on my lifestyle.

Along with thousands of other names, who were similarly clear they had been dishonestly dealt with, I joined every 'action group' in sight, and which had been set up to defend ourselves. From time to time a name who felt aggrieved over some aspect of his membership had challenged Lloyds, but with their virtually unlimited funds, they invariably saw the plaintiff off. Initially Lloyd's response was arrogantly dismissive, but they had never, in their three hundred years' existence, been faced with literally thousands of united names bent on securing justice, and whose collective pocket rivalled Lloyds.

The best lawyers were recruited, and there began a legal war that was to last some years. Court case followed court case, and without exception we won them all. Lloyds retreated and offered a thousand million pounds to ease names liabilities. This was rejected out of hand. More court cases, more victories. Lloyds, now thoroughly chastened, returned with a fresh offer of almost three thousand millions. This time most names accepted, and moved into a run off insurance vehicle formed for the purpose. I finally agreed a settlement figure which left me with a loss of about ten thousand as a result of my dalliance with that once great institution, and that included the three thousand joining fee. With that I could live! It began to be said of Lloyds that those wealthy enough to join were wealthy enough not to! Ah well, hindsight is the only twenty/twenty vision! The traditional 'name' who accepted unlimited liability is now almost a thing of the past.

A few years ago, as I approached seventy, the children took over the running of G.F., and have proved much wiser and steadier in the management of it. They bottom out the risk profile with a thoroughness that would do justice to a clearing bank. The profits bear witness to the wisdom of their approach. Their several skills are almost tailor-made for operating such a business. Mark, certainly so far, has generated most of the business, but then sales and marketing were always his strengths. Anne, supported off stage by her husband Chris, has an intimate and detailed knowledge of the property world, an area that forms the bulk of the company' s lending. Richard deals with all the legal aspects and controls the accounts and paperwork. Mandy deploys her journalistic skills taking minutes, etc. Though neither a director nor shareholder, I am allowed to sit in at the board meetings, and chirp up from time to time. Now, of what profession was it always said that it enjoyed influence without responsibility!

My mother had died some years previously, having reached her middle eighties and been a widow for a quarter of a century. The old family home, with its stairs, had been sold some time previously, and she had settled into an attractive, quietly situated bungalow very comfortably. Her very strong personality had been the hand on the tiller throughout our childhood years. It was she who had created the framework of our lives, and given us the values that informed all we did. Family, particularly her two children, were her all, and we owed her much for that.

This later proved to be a problem. When I married, there had to be a change of precedence. A wife must come before a mother, but this was something that she was never properly able, right up to the end, to come to terms with. This resentment inevitably damaged her relationship with me, and wasn't helped when it became clear that Judy was at least as capable a manager and mother as she had been herself. Had Judy needed to depend on her, that might have made a difference, but she didn't and wouldn't, for Judy had picked up the vibes of resentment and had no problem in distancing herself from someone who found it difficult to be genuinely and warmly agreeable.

Through the years, a surface friendliness obtained, reciprocal visits and meals continued, and most Christmases were spent with us. Because my office was close to where she lived, I made it my business to pop in at least once a week, check all was well and have a chat and a cup of coffee. I made sure her income was adjusted from time to time as inflation ate away at its value, and, having sold the business, included her in the gain. None of this altered the overall picture. She would only have been satisfied if she had been in control, making the decisions, the way it had been in the past. This could not be. There was one occasion, when complaining that she didn't see enough of us, I pointed out that she saw a lot more of me than I saw of my own children, who had by this time moved away! I might as well have saved my breath. As time moved on, my weekly visits became duty rather than pleasure, but continued to the end.

Perhaps there was some gain from all this, for it underlined to us that parents do not own their children. They are stewards for a season, whose task is to prepare them for the real world they will in due time face, and then release them to become what they will. That business of releasing is almost certainly the most demanding part of parenting. Beginning as teenagers, much reliance has to be placed on the values given in the earlier years, for these will be needed to steer them clear of catastrophe as they start to make decisions for themselves. This underlines just how vital are those early years of induction. How quickly, in what areas first, do you let go? Each must work it out for himself or herself—there are no degree courses in parenting. But let go one must, and if this is done, there is every chance there will be a relaxed and happy relationship with one's sometime, now no longer, children. The relationship will have moved on from stewardship to friendship.

Some years previously Judy had indicated that it would make sense for us to move south, nearer to where the children and grandchildren were based. For my part I just couldn't contemplate leaving Gawsworth. To square the circle, and for several years, I hired a flat for about eighty days a year in a small apartment block in Draycott Av., in London. This worked well, enabling Judy to spend several days a month there and making whatever arrangements she chose to see the family. However, it was decided to buy a flat in Islington, only minutes' walk from both Richard and Anne's offices. Once the family were in a position to look after it, and be responsible for its care and maintenance, I was quite relaxed about it. What I had earlier resisted was a London place for which I had to be responsible. This allows Judy to spend more or less whatever time she wishes there. So the pressure to move is off!

IN RETROSPECT

In all of life there is a beginning and an end. That which has a beginning must also have an ending. For me, my commercial life ended in August 2003, when I retired from a company called Bespokes, which was in the process of substantially changing its spots. The two chief shareholders were both friends—Mario Budwig and Bill Holroyd. I had done business with Mario through G.F. and, of course, Bill was an old friend of some duration. The rationale behind my becoming chairman was very simple. Both parties were very strong characters, both knew me well, and both agreed to my holding the ring in the event of a major disagreement! (There can be quite surprising reasons for appointing a chairman!) In the event there were no such problems, and for the rest, it would have to be allowed that my input was very modest.

In retrospect, it has all passed so quickly. I have loved my work, each and every part of it. Even the crises, and there have been several of those, for a crisis overcome leaves an afterglow of exhilaration. Building and development is tremendously satisfying. Whether it is a new factory, or a house, or a block of flats, the sense that it is happening because one started the ball rolling, took the initiative, is hugely stimulating. But it was the laundry, later workwear rental business, that was the most satisfying. It was a people-intensive game, and it is always people that matter, that are interesting, and that are challenging.

Working, as always had to be the case, within the unforgiving framework of a competitive world, the only way materially more could be done for a workforce was if they could be motivated and enabled to achieve more. Much of my time was given to trying to find ways of bringing about such motivation. Was I successful? Some progress in the right direction, yes. But not, by any means, complete success. Suspicion of the capitalist system was perhaps too deeply ingrained in that sector of the community from which my people came. All the plants I had were based in Greater Merseyside, possibly the most militant part of the U.K. Our workers' husbands, wives or parents were invariably strong trade unionists. Every move by management was questioned, and it would have been folly to hope that some acknowledgement of effort would have been made. Possibly the nearest thing to an endorsement I ever received was when, after about a year of

Baynes involvement, a co-ordinated approach was made by my people to ask me to return! And a second one after about two years!

Whilst I have spent time on the boards of three quoted companies, and in the case of Charles Baynes for a dozen years, at heart I have always been a small company man. In my own business, I never employed more than a hundred and fifty people, and after moving to our new premises, the efficiencies that were realisable there, together with some quantum leaps in new machines and systems, got that number closer to a hundred. At that sort of size you know everybody, and communications are more easily maintained. If there is a matter of importance, it is possible to talk to the whole payroll at one go. Small companies can respond more quickly to change. There is an immediacy and a bracing quality that is very stimulating. Even big, quoted companies can go bust, but small ones are always much nearer the abyss, and that concentrates the mind!

As my commercial affairs wound gently down, it became possible to spend more time on alternatives. Reading had always been a number one interest, now much expanded, wide ranging and eclectic, a side effect being the need for periodic additions to bookshelves to house a now two and a half thousand volumes! The piano too has had more attention in recent years, though the results remain very modest, and I've had to recognize that I will never be able to tackle any really demanding work. Gardening in small quantities is very agreeable, rather like cleaning shoes—the result of one's labour is rewardingly visible! To have to do it routinely, though, would, it may he imagined, quickly cause it to become an onerous chore. Walking or rambling, usually in company with a group from the church, is an agreeable way to spend a few hours, though up to half a dozen miles is now the limit of my comfort zone!

Quite a lot of time gets consumed on church affairs. P.C.C., Deanery and Diocesan Synods, and Bishop's Council all take time. It might be that the church, being the sort of organisation it is, has found that these various gatherings are the best way to manage its business. My own experience argues that meetings which involve dozens of people, and in the case of the Diocesan Synod, over a hundred, achieve little. They are hugely costly in time, achieve painfully inadequate results, and do so incredibly slowly. The comparison with a commercial organisation, with a turnover of many hundreds of millions, a payroll measured in thousands, and run by a main board of half a dozen, is dire.

A more rewarding activity as that of a Reader (in Anglican terminology, a 'Reader' is a layman licensed to take services, etc.), and this has tended to increase. In the local area and in the context of a small group of churches, I find myself taking about forty services a year. The real gain is the need to give time to preparation. This in turn keeps one's mind active, an important consideration for someone several years in the departure lounge of life! Readers take services by invitation only, so there is an incentive to keep on one's toes, else the invites can be expected to dry up! Then there is the Study Group I started and which has met monthly at my home for the past eight or more years. Five of our members are now able to, and do, lead. These are supplemented by outside speakers from time to time. The name of the group consciously excludes the word 'bible', for whilst there are sessions of bible exposition and study, the net is cast wider to include any area that may help the growth of those who attend.

There is a paradox in life. Three quarters of it is spent trying to win a place in the sun, of gaining sufficient to make it possible to carry through those things that have the highest priority, such as in our case, the education of our children. The remaining quarter it all goes into reverse. Those priorities have either been accomplished or abandoned, and with increasing evidence that one is mortal, the need to start shedding surplus assets becomes very real. Andrew Carnegie once said, "It is a disgrace for a man to die rich." Whilst in today's terms I have never been that, nonetheless, he has a point. For some time therefore I have been reducing my position, largely in favour of the children. In such matters it would be enormously helpful in planning to know just how much time is left!

"Largely in favour of the children"—but not entirely. Giving is surely an important element of life. No matter how wealthy he may be, no man is so poor as he who cannot give. As in so many other areas of life, it helps to take an ordered approach. For Christians, the scriptural guidance is that it is acceptable to spend ten pounds on oneself for every pound given away. This would seem to he weighting the scales very much in favour of the donor. Not so. Overall, the U.K. has a G.N.P. of a little over a trillion (£1,000,000,000,000) or a thousand billions. Total annual giving in this country is around six or seven billion pounds or .6 or .7 of 1%. Clearly, not too many share the scriptural view!

For my own part, as my income came to depend significantly on capital movements, a traditional approach didn't work very well. In my worst year, for example, my 'income' was a six figure minus! In such a case it really isn't practical to ask the various charities to return the previous year's donations! For many years now I have therefore worked on actual expenditure, and expect to donate £10 for every £100 spent on ourselves and our affairs. Gifts to immediate family obviously don't count for this purpose.

As noted earlier, we have eleven grandchildren, though little else has been said about them. They are: Amy, Lucy, Hugh, Alice, Georgia, Charles, James, David, Sarah, Jack, and last in appearance, Edward. Ranging in age from 5 to17, each is a unique person, no two alike! Raising our own four, we were very close to the action; now, in more leisured fashion, we watch the emerging characters and personalities of each with enormous (but hopefully without interfering!) interest. What will each become, who will they link up with, how will they deal with the inevitable challenges this life unfailingly throws up? Nearly all remains yet to unfold, but in these our later years, it is a source of great interest and hope, and we love them every one.

So far only Amy, now seventeen, the eldest of the eleven, has given a future career indication. She has long had an interest in photography, and when she entered a national competition and won the first prize, £2k of photographic equipment, this quickened her thoughts about making it a career. A further push came when out of 10,000 entrants, her pictures were short listed into one of the twenty-eight finalists, the winner yet to he determined. What did quickly become apparent, and was a matter of very real joy to us, was that all the parents had the same determination to give their children the very best education and encouragement, and which had informed our own decisions a generation earlier.

My paternal grandfather had three boys; they in turn between them had three sons. Those three managed only two, our sons Mark and Richard, and now the latest generation is back to three, in the shape of Mark's three sons! The Clegg label would seem to be likely therefore to survive for at least a further period!

Little has been said here about the golden thread that has run through almost my entire life, and that is the faith that has sustained me. It has long been clear that this life could not reasonably be the whole. We are so made that the idea of an arbitrary end that renders everything ultimately meaningless, is just not reasonable. If this life isn't the whole, then what is?

Firstly, there's the evidence for a creative intelligence, of an order beyond our comprehension. Most reasonable people would agree that the inventor has a higher level of intelligence than the man who comes along later to find out how he did it. Many tens of thousands of the finest brains over the last few centuries have spent their entire lives discovering cumulatively a little of how the universe, and in particular our own planet, was devised and is governed. Given this, the devising intelligence must be of a quite extraordinary order. That the intelligence is one and undivided, is evidenced by the harmony and interlocking character of the law governing the universe, and which science unfailingly demonstrates.

But, it follows logically, that such intelligence would be interested in, and have a purpose for that creation, and more particularly, the highest and most complex aspect of it, man. Being such, we are entitled to ask, and expect to know, what that purpose is. It has been the function of the great world religions to set out to answer that question. Stripping out the oceans of self-serving and power oriented responses that are the baggage of them all, there remains a residue. That residue is love (love is that which seeks a person's best) and truth. Both are eternal, nothing else is. All the big five (Hinduism, Judaism, Buddhism, Christianity and Islam) are, at the level of their mystics, saying essentially the same thing, though it seems to me Christianity speaks with the greatest clarity. It follows therefore that our task, as sons of this intelligence—'God' is a useful shorthand—is to practice the one and absorb the other. Sons? Indeed we have to be of the essence of this God, like Him in all essentials. Were it not so, we couldn't conceive of Him, speak to Him, or know Him. Similarly, we must have proceeded from Him, for there is only God.

That I am, along with the six billion other human beings presently on the planet, a son of God, seems to me therefore self evident. In the ordinary day-to-day world we inhabit, especially in areas where every lift of an eyebrow is recognised for what it means, such as at home and work, demonstrating the relationship we have with this God by what we do, must surely be the key. Let that he done, and words will, most of the time, be superfluous. If that isn't done, words will prove a poor substitute. The Chinese have a proverb: "I can't hear what you say, your deeds are shouting so loud."

If the history of nations is, in large measure, the history of war, then the record of individuals is extensively a tally of their mistakes and failures. As I look back over my life, it isn't hard to note a durable tendency to get it wrong, or a multitude of points at which a better response or wiser decision might have been made. But from such we learn, and must keep on learning. All of this allowed, it's been great to have lived, to have been given the privilege of having "A Life".

END

0-595-34300-7

Lightning Source UK Ltd.
Milton Keynes UK
02 August 2010

157801UK00001B/34/A